Hey Buddy…
Dubious Advice from Dad
by
nathan timmel

For Truman

(of course)

June 1

Hey Buddy…

You have reached a milestone, and I am sorry.

A few short weeks ago, Mommy or I would put you in your crib and you'd mewl for a minute, maybe two. After that you'd think, "Oh, what the hell? I'm tired. Might as well go to sleep and not bother with all the noise."

And that was that.

Now, not only are you aware of being left behind, you know all too well what happens to Mommy and Daddy at bedtime. You are aware that after laying you down, we exit through the door in your room. Maybe you always saw this, but now you realize it.

Therein lies the difference.

This new consciousness, combined with your recent attempts to crawl, has led to a wonderfully sad, heartbreaking period for you: separation anxiety. You now realize that not only are Mommy and Daddy (and Sister and Doggy) somewhere else in the house, but that you could join us if you could only get out of your crib and through the door.

Last night I placed you in your crib, and you were unhappy.

I gave you a kiss on the forehead and stole away, expecting the usual scenario: a minute of crying, followed by the silence of your slumber.

Except, after two minutes you were still crying. Same with three minutes. Same with five minutes.

I tippy-toed back to your room, gently cracked the door and peered in... and you were not where I had left you.

I had laid you down head facing away from the door, far side of the crib. When I checked back in, you were sitting up, corner of the crib, right next to the door. You were so sad about being left alone that you moved your little body to the last place you saw Daddy: exiting the room.

Once there, you were trapped by the bars of your bed. All you could do was grasp them and howl.

Of course I immediately opened the door wide, stepped in and reached down to scoop you up. You instinctively grabbed at me, clawed at me, signaling your need for contact, trying to climb into my arms as I lifted you.

Daddy's warmth > the empty crib.

I carried you back into the living room and your tears slowed, eventually halting entirely. Mommy and I still cannot figure out whether or not you weren't tired enough for bed, or if it was just another case of FOMO—fear of missing out—from you.

For a few weeks now, we've suspected FOMO weighs heavy on you. Sometimes, when Mommy or I carry you into your room for nap or bedtime, you start to fuss. You know what's coming and want nothing to do with it.

If the fussing turns to a full-on tantrum, the mere gesture of bringing you back through the door and into the hallway ends your tears; they shut off as if by spigot. You know all too well the difference between your bedroom and the "social rooms" of the house.

In your bedroom, you're left alone. In the living room? Oh, there's so much going on, so much to do. Action aplenty, so to speak. In your room, you miss out on everything going on while you sleep, and that is unacceptable.

More often than not, that second burst of love is all you need. Ten extra minutes hanging out with the family. Five extra minutes of smiling at your sister. Three bonus minutes of flailing at Doggy in an attempt to pet him. It's a reminder that we are always somewhere close, and that you're never truly abandoned.

Then we second-attempt to put you to bed, and it usually works.

Hopefully, before long you will pass the next milestone, where you don't even need that bonus trip to the living room.

Hopefully, before long you will understand that you are always loved, even when Mommy and Daddy are not in the room with you.

Hopefully, before long, you will sleep serenely.

Hopefully.

Love,

Dad

August 14

Hey Buddy...

I am in Livonia, Michigan, thinking about an article Mommy sent me.

The story discussed babies and brainwaves, and the focus was Russian children turned sociopaths. A study discovered that if orphaned at birth — depending on their circumstances — certain babies would sit in their crib and cry. Which is normal; babies cry. But if the orphanage had too few workers, and no caretaker arrived to soothe the infant for hours and then days, the baby's brain waves were so affected by the trauma that they shut down. They "learned" at a very, very young age to go neutral as a form of self-preservation. As they aged, the children were emotionally "dead," with no concern for other people; they had no empathy in them.

It was one of the most depressing things I have ever read.

When you were four months old, you woke up, agitated, at 1:26 AM. You got a couple of short bursts out as I stole into your room as quickly as possible. Before your mewling could turn into a storm, I knelt by your crib, slipped an arm between two slats, and caressed your head.

Your fussing stopped immediately.

Immediately.

Your legs stopped kicking, your arms ceased their flailing, and you relaxed into the mattress, your eyes closed.

There is something incredibly powerful and humbling about being able to pacify an infant simply by giving it the skin-to-skin contact of your hand. A baby may not know much, but it knows warmth, and love. The reaction to a gentle touch is instinctive; there are no words needed to explain what goes through a baby's tiny brain at that moment: I was scared and alone, but now someone is here. I am safe.

As you sighed peacefully back to sleep, I felt overwhelming love mixed with immense sorrow.

Sorrow because…

Well, let me explain it like this: when you buy a car, suddenly you notice that particular car everywhere on the road. Now that I'm a parent, almost every day I stumble across news articles involving the abuse of an infant or child. I'm sure those stories were always in the news, but now they leap out at me.

Maybe my brain is wired incorrectly, but as I knelt beside you, your tiny head eclipsed by the palm of my hand, the thought of Russian babies crying, with no one able or attempting to calm them made my heart sink. Call me weak, but I am not a parent that can allow my baby to "cry it out."

As your sister, or "Sister" as you know her, ages, I allow her to explore and get "hurt" more often. Today when she falls, I smile and compliment her, saying something idiotic, like "Good job, sweetie!" The idea being that she will take her cues from me, and if I am not alarmed by her stumbles, she won't be, either. When she was an infant, however, and confined to a crib? I would tend to her the instant her whimpering began.

10

Just like I do for you.

When you become a parent, that is your duty; you must care for your child. When you become a parent, your life is over in the best way possible. Instead of living inside the ego of "me, me, me," you make peace with the simple truth that you must provide for another.

The idea anyone could not live up to that duty, that anyone could neglect or abandon an infant, or harm a child... I cannot wrap my head around it. The knowledge there are people who actively hurt children... I tell you this: show me someone who hurts the defenseless, and I will show you the reason I have trouble believing in God. But that is neither here nor there.

With you sleeping peacefully once again, I decided to ease back my hand and exit the room. As I was closing the door, I took one final look down and wondered what had disturbed you in the first place. A nightmare? A noise? While it is a mystery I will never solve, in a flash a thought crossed my mind that wiped away all the negativity I had been swimming in.

Probably misses his old glasses.

I had to stifle a laugh, lest I wake you again. There are few things in life a Simpsons reference cannot fix, and I promise to explain that one to you.

Love,

Dad

August 20

Hey Buddy...

As I write, you are one, and your sister is three.

All summer, I've been taking the two of you to either the local playground, or, when the mercury brushes up against the 90-degree notch and humidity hovers around one million percent, to an indoor squishy-floored play area. While doing this, I have noticed three basic parent types:

- The Helicopter, standing over their child at all times with a protective hand always waiting for a fall of any kind, even a harmless drop of inches.

- The Cell Phone, nose-deep in whatever electronic device is in their palm, their kids whooping it up attention-free.

- The Interactive, who is playing and laughing along with their kids.

The last is somewhat rare; you can stumble across one or two, but not very often. I am an interactive parent, and without meaning to, I occasionally embarrass other adults at the playground.

When at a park, I run around and climb structures with Sister. "Daddy sit here!" is her laughing battle cry as she asks me to plop down next to her on a double slide.

When at the indoor squishy play area, I'm on the floor with you, allowing you to bear crawl after me under bridges and through tunnels. You laugh with glee the whole time, especially when I turn around and tickle-attack after you "catch" me.

Cell Phone parents watch this somewhat ashamedly, the thought, "Should I be doing that, too?" written across their faces. The embarrassment grows when their kids take note of the laughter and joy encircling my kids and me, and rush over. Sometimes they stand on the periphery of joy, a hesitant smile asking, "Can I join in?" Other times I have been playfully tackled by children I've never met; they decided then and there they were going to enter the fray, caution be damned.

I watch as Cell Phone parents grow uncomfortable. They put the electronics away and do their clumsy-best to play with their child, which tends to look like someone on a first date.

Their fear is palpable, and "If I get down on all fours and crawl around, I'll look silly" shows in their body language. Sometimes they try to maintain an air of composure while playing, which makes them look all the more silly, but you know what? It doesn't matter to their kid. No matter how embarrassed the adult feels, every single time I see one of them start interacting with their child, the child's face lights up like Christmas morning.

I became an Interactive Parent by accident. One day Sister and I showed up at a play area before anyone else. She was around two-years-old, so as she waddle-walked around and attempted her best to climb everything, I joined her. I made silly faces, pounded my hands on whatever was available for hand-pounding, and did whatever possible to keep her amused.

When other kids arrived I backed off a bit, allowing her to make friends. Every so often, however, I noticed her glancing over at me. Ostensibly she wanted to make sure I was there, but more subtly I think she wanted to make sure I was still paying attention to her. Every time our eyes locked, she'd smile. I'd smile back, and then she'd go back about her important toddler business.

As I looked around and saw other parents lost in their phones, I wondered what their kids thought when they searched for parental approval. Probably nothing, but over an extended period the idea "The phone is more important than me" could creep in.

With that, I decided to be conscious about phone use when out with the two of you. When I can, I leave it in the car so I'm not even tempted to play around.

There are always nostalgic cries about "the way things used to be," as well as complaints involving "kids these days," but sensibilities aren't formed in a vacuum. Parents guide kids, and parents have changed. Adults are as distracted as kids now, either working or killing time on their electronic devices constantly.

Which I get. Taking a child to the park can be as much a respite for the parent as it is playtime for the child. Parenting is hard, but to borrow from Jimmy Dugan: "The hard is what makes it great."

If society wants to say "kids are different," then society has to take a long look in the mirror. You and Sister might grow up to be hyperactive little monsters that I failed to raise correctly, but it won't be from lack of effort. If anything, I'm going to fail you by putting in too much effort. Because, to be honest, I'm making this up as I go along.

But I'm loving it.

Love,

Dad

September 1

Hey Buddy...

Babies are easy.

I know, because you just turned one. When it is time to do something I just pick you up, cart you around like a football, and go about my business. When it is time for a bath, I run some warm water, place you in it, and scrub you down.

You, for the record, giggle and enjoy it. Sister, however, just turned three, and she is... well, challenging is a polite way to put it.

She used to love baths, like you currently do. She'd sit in the water, happily splashing, giggling, and occasionally attempting to stand and knock her noggin on the spigot.

Now, depending on her temperament, getting her into the tub can be a chore in and of itself.

Shouts of "Nooooooo! I no wanna!" sound forth from her throat like Whitman's barbaric yawp; she protests as if the tub were filled with live snakes and not tepid bathwater. Arms and legs flail as if auditioning for The Exorcist.

Bribes — innocuous nothings like, "But it has bubbles!" and "Look at all the toys in there!" — are offered, but usually fail more quickly than an abstinence-only lecture on prom night.

Sometimes Mommy and I attempt a stern approach—"You are going to take a bath!"—which of course never works and only upsets her further.

In fact, nothing seems to succeed when the tears and thrashing starts. Then, it's all over...

...until something uniquely absurd fires across the synapses of Sister's wee mind. Only when her own distinctive brand of creativity takes place does tub-time—which is like Hammer Time, only without the puffy pants—occur.

"I want bath with Kitty."

Kitty.

Our Miniature Schnauzer. Sister wants to take a bath with the dog.

As a parent, you come across unreasonable demands, and reasonable-yet-awkward demands. I found this to be the latter. If I can avoid a fight, I will. And so, on that particularly joyous day I picked up Kitty and placed him in the tub with Sister.

The two reactions could not have been more different. Sister was overjoyed; her smile spread ear-to-ear. Kitty... well, he looked at me in a manner that suggested if he could roll his eyes, he would have. In fact, since you and Sister have joined the family, his look has been one that suggests "Someone call SPCA." Because while you and Sister love him, your muscle control isn't the best. When you try to pet him lovingly, you flail and bat at him instead. And Sister? Let's just say she's getting in more kissing practice than she needs using the dog.

The dog isn't the only creature to suffer under our roof; I too have had to "take one for the team," so to speak. During one exciting tantrum involving bath time, the perfectly intoned words "I want Daddy in the tub" exited Sister's mouth.

Daddy. Me.

I am 6'2" and 183 pounds of blubber. Bathtubs are not made for someone of my size. I cannot comfortably sit alone in a household bathtub, much less squeeze into one with another person, even if that other person is pint-sized.

But, if it will put an end to the tantrum, I will do what I can. And I tell you this: it is amazing how quickly a toddler can go from "possessed by Satan" to ecstatic.

It has long been said that a person should pick and choose their battles, and when it comes to "You do not take a bath with the dog!" or "Whatever, Kitty, come here," I'm not interested in that fight. Likewise, the "I want Daddy in the tub" battle.

Toddlers are irrational little people. You can fight them, or join them. I choose not to take arms against a sea of troubles, I let be.

And as of now, I am enjoying your happy demeanor and your willingness to simply acquiesce and slip into warm, bubbled water without protest.

But my eyes are forever on the future, and I already loathe the day you begin your terrible twos.

Love,

Dad

September 10

Hey Buddy...

I am in Colorado Springs, sleeping all by my lonesome for a couple of nights. Most parents revel in solitude, but I do not.

Somewhere around the time Sister turned two, she figured out how to turn a doorknob.

Being in the 98th percentile height-wise made it easy for her nimble little fingers to reach the blessed thing easily. That she figured out how to turn it so early on was just a testament to her clever, miniature mind.

The interesting thing is: she didn't use her newfound ability to Houdini her way out of the bedroom right away. Upon learning our daughter could enter and exit rooms at will, Mommy and I thought our restful evenings were over. We figured she would suddenly be up all night, every night, wandering the house and enjoying her newfound toddler freedom. But that didn't happen.

About six months later, however, Sister had a light bulb moment. She realized that not only could she open her door, she also knew where Mommy and Daddy slept.

Combining these two thoughts, she came stumbling into the master bedroom one night around 3am. Mommy sleeps closest to the door, so she was the one greeted by our groggy girl. Mommy was able to settle the wee one back into her own room without trouble, but two-year-olds are nothing if not tenacious. Soon Sister was waddling her way into our room once a week. Waters were being tested; big (relatively speaking) toes were being dipped. Even thought she might not have been intentionally searching for boundaries, I do believe she was instinctively doing so.

Sister was about to realize something she already knew, that under our roof, Daddy is the softie.

After several entries that resulted in rejection via Mommy, she tried a new approach: Sister snuck into the room, crawled into bed on Daddy's side, and sprawled herself across my chest.

Instead of picking her up and returning her to her own bed, I snuggled her tight and covered her with a blanket.

She popped a thumb in her mouth, and fell back asleep.

Safe.

Warm.

(I spent the next several hours being kicked and farted on. But I didn't mind.)

That started, in biblical terms, the end of days.

What began as 5 a.m. or 3 a.m. once-a-week intrusions became 11 p.m. and 10 p.m. attempts nightly. Sister came into our room earlier and earlier, and more and more often.

Like before, if Mommy was awake (or awoke first), back to the toddler room she went. But when able to enter and make her way to me, I always allowed her to snuggle in and disrupt my sleep.

This created a slight... let's say bone of contention, between Mommy and me. She likes to read parenting books, and talks at length about conditioning and bad habits. Which I understand. I also don't care.

Sister is three.

In my mind, she'll be thirteen tomorrow.

Time is fleeting. I don't know how long snuggling lasts; how long she'll want to come cuddle with me. I know that when she's a teenager, I'll be the most embarrassing thing in her life and that she'll want little to do with me.

These moments are precious, and I don't want to waste them. If Sister wants snuggles and warmth in the middle of the night, who am I to deny her?

Mommy has stated — a stern look upon her face — that she isn't looking forward to the day you, currently one and ever-clever when it comes to working through and around obstacles in your way, figure out how to meander into our room.

"If she isn't able to stay in her own room by then, our bed will be too crowded! Two kids, us, and a dog? That's too much!"

To Mommy, but not to me. It's a day I'm actually looking forward to.

Snuggling with the two of you sounds like heaven to me.

Love,

Dad

September 17

Hey Buddy...

Sometimes you need all your dinosaur friends at breakfast.

September 25

Hey Buddy…

I am in La Crosse, Wisconsin.

Over the course of my career, I've had the honor of performing for American troops stationed far from home. I've been in the war zones of Iraq and Afghanistan, and the beautiful countries of Japan and Korea—just to name a few. Maybe someday you'll be leafing through one of our many photo albums, see some shots of me in a Black Hawk helicopter or surrounded by cherry trees in blossom, and ask what all that was about.

That point may come before this letter hits your hands, but I want to share something with you that I wrote several years back.

I tell jokes for a living, which means that generally, I make people happy. But every so often I'm afforded the opportunity to make them reflect. I don't realize it in the moment, but after they explain that I reached them emotionally? Well, it's quite humbling.

Here's one such tale.

* * *

"Just give them a good show, sweetie. You never know who'll be in the audience."

Those words are sounding inside me as I stare uncomfortably at the doe-eyed woman I have been conversing with. A petite five-foot-nothing, she is charmingly pretty, and starting to tear up as she struggles to express herself. Unfortunately, everything has grown awkward quickly, mainly due to my inability to take a hint, be even marginally aware of my surroundings, or have any grace whatsoever when it comes to the verbal ballet necessary when emotions are involved.

I hate being so dense.

* * *

I am in the Upper Peninsula of Michigan, Sault Saint Marie. It's the tippity-top of America and a stone's throw from the Canadian border. I am performing at a casino, which is always a crapshoot; when people go out to gamble, a comedy show isn't always on their radar. That I am in the casino bar makes things worse. Here you have those who are taking a break from gambling... or even worse, dejected souls who have run through their money and are drinking away their losses. Neither makes for an ideal audience.

REO Speedwagon is playing the main theater, making me realize I went my whole life without knowing that Northern Michigan is where rock goes to die. I am telling my wife of the competition, and she shoots the quote that opened this story my way. I smile into the phone and tell her that no matter what happens, I'm OK with it. Hell, the night prior only fourteen people showed up, but they were fourteen attentive, laughter-filled folks who came to have a good time. Truth be told, I'd much rather have fourteen happy people at my show than 200 indifferent ones.

As it turns out, the casino has scheduled the two events back-to-back; comedy is to begin just after the dying echo of Keep on Loving You fades into the air. Somewhere in the hotel I picture a clever manager giving himself a shoulder-chuck à la Anthony Michael Hall in The Breakfast Club.

28

That person knew what he was doing, because a healthy throng of people migrates directly from the theater to the bar, and as the first comic goes up it's standing room only. The crowd is large; they are drinking, relaxing, and most importantly, laughing.

Soon it is my turn upon the stage, and without going into details it's just one of those nights. Everything works, everything hits. Laughter, applause, more laughter, more applause...

When I hit my contracted time I'm tempted to linger and extend the show. I admit my ego is weak and screams for more attention on nights like this. I consider basking in the sun of my personal Sally Field moment a bit longer — I've got the material; I could fire off stories for over 90 minutes if I wanted — but decide against doing so. As much fun as I'm having, the major drawback to the world of slot machines and poker-bluffs is that you can still smoke within its walls. Plumes of blue-gray cigarette smoke have been exhaled forth all evening, and over the course of the previous hour I've bathed in it. I can feel it infesting my pores and laying cancerous eggs. I want a shower more than anything else.

With a goodnight wave I leave the stage; better to leave them wanting more than giving too much. In the back of my mind is the niggling little fact that many casinos don't like shows to run long. Every minute a person isn't on the gaming floor is, well, another minute they're not on the gaming floor. The logic behind that should be beyond self-evident even to the most dimwitted among us.

I stand behind the table I've set my wares upon, and happily enough, folks are coming by with cash in hand. They're a little intoxicated, they've laughed — it's a perfect combination for me to help them part with a portion of their paycheck.

I begin singing The Banana Splits song to myself; each sale becomes another fruit to me: "One banana, two banana, three banana, four..."

Customers come, customers go; smiles, handshakes, transactions. This is repeated until only one woman remains. She has been waiting patiently at the back of the line, and I turn to acknowledge her.

"Hi," I smile. "Did you have fun tonight?"

"Yes," she responds with a sad smile, giving me pause.

She extends her left hand.

I quickly realize my phone is in my right hand, set it down, and smilingly extend a greeting her way.

She extends her right hand, but leaves her left forward.

As I am an idiot, I now take both hands, and shake them heartily. In my mind, I am imagining Buster Keaton and Groucho Marx; this is exactly what they would do in such a situation. It's playful, right?

After a moment, I return her appendages and she looks at me, slightly frustrated.

"No..." she explains, and offers her left hand yet again.

Within a span of seconds I say the word "Oh" twice. First, an upbeat, oh, I get it now! You're offering me your left hand for a reason! Almost immediately following is an "Oh" of realization. It is the release of air, one combined with a sinking feeling and accompanied by the words "shit" or "my God."

On her wrist is a small, black metallic band. It looks fused in place, like it is never meant to be removed. Etched upon it is a name.

A name, and a date.

A soldier.

On stage, I am very vocal about my support for the men and women of the United States military. I tell tales of my nine tours overseas to provide laughter to the men and women serving in places like Iraq and Afghanistan. I do not delve into politics; I keep things close to the vest, discussing the human aspect to everything. No matter anyone's feelings on war, government, or any political affiliations, behind the uniform is a person. A mother. Father. Wife.

In the case of this woman, a husband.

My embarrassed eyes looked away too quickly to remember the name, but I believe the day this woman lost her husband was in 2009.

She begins thanking me for my tours, telling me how much it means to her the troops are remembered and supported.

That humans are selfish is no secret; I was in Iraq in 2009. As she speaks I think back to my time there and wonder if I had against all odds stumbled across her husband. I have shaken thousands of hands while on military bases. Was his one of them?

The most difficult part of any war-zone comedy tour is honoring gratitude. I have had shows cancelled due to incoming mortars. I have flown over mountaintops in open-door helicopters, the air so frigid I began to turn numb. I have waited countless hours in airports and on planes, performed in awkward, improvised locations, and slept in the worst of beds with the most stinky of sleeping bags. It's what I sign up for, and is to be expected. But when a man or woman whose life is on the line every single day, who has been stationed far from home for months or years takes hold of my hand, looks me dead in the eye and thanks me for my little dog and pony show, that's where I stumble.

I do my best to listen to the woman telling me how important it is to the men and women serving that they are remembered, but am torn. I understand I have to respect her words, but part of me wants to scream at the top of my lungs: "Don't thank me, I do nothing! I fly in, strut and fret my hour upon the stage, and am heard no more! You have suffered real loss!"

I remain silent and feel guilty for feeling guilty. Emotions of self-disgust swirl inside me, making me wish I could accept simple thanks without my mind wandering down a path of world injustices and karmic failure.

Maybe she has been drinking, maybe she is truly overcome with emotions too troubling to hold in, but soon she is reduced to a refrain of "Thank you... your words about supporting our troops meant so much. Thank you... thank you..."

A large part of me wants to give her a hug, draw her tightly to me as if my embrace could somehow give her a moment's respite from the pain. I don't for two reasons. One, I don't know this woman. It would be unfair of me to impose my will upon her in response to the current situation. And therein lies my second reason for not reaching out: when I am overcome with emotion I absolutely do not want to be touched. I prefer being left to my own devices to deal with whatever I'm going through, and physical contact repulses me in the moment. What if she holds a somewhat similar disposition?

32

As I do not know her specific kinks, I do not invade her personal space. In the end, all I can do is offer a free CD, telling her the material she enjoyed is on the disc.

She leaves me by backing away, repeating over and over how much my words meant. Her eyes are watery, but no actual tears flow.

You never know who will be in your audience.

*   *   *

Buddy, the last line is important, because you can exchange "audience" with "life."

You never know who the stranger is in front of you. You don't know their story, their baggage, the struggles they've overcome.

I have found it's best to greet everyone from a point of equality, and openness.

I hope to impart that lesson upon you, that you may live your life full of empathy.

Love,

Dad

October 3

Hey Buddy...

Because she loves you—and Sister—Mommy was a bit of a "breastfeeding Nazi." To be fair, I suppose she remains one. Breastfeeding is something Mommy is quite passionate about.

That said, even though nursing has been scientifically (and repeatedly) proven the best/healthiest way to feed a baby, sometimes there are legitimate reasons for a mother not to do it.

Maybe she has flat nipples and the baby can't latch, or her employer offers no maternity leave or pumping breaks (welcome to America: first-world country with third-world women's rights). Maybe the parents adopted, and getting donor breast milk is an enormous pain in the tuckus.

(There are more, but you get the point.)

On the flip side, there are also illegitimate reasons, such as "I didn't want to," "I tried for all of one minute but the baby wouldn't latch so I gave up," and my favorite, "I was afraid it would ruin my breasts."

Those aside, the most absurd reason I've heard not to nurse is one that offended me as a dad: "I didn't want my husband to feel excluded."

I read an article where a mother decided that nursing created too intimate a bond between her and the baby, one the father couldn't compete with. To level the playing field, each would bottle feed.

It wasn't an April Fool's joke, and the article wasn't trolling — being outrageous just for the sake of getting people fired up. The woman actually believed it would be unfair to her husband if she nursed, and therefore bonded more closely with her child than he could.

It would take a thesaurus to list the words describing how idiotic that line of reasoning is. I put it on par with "Iraq has WMDs" and "vaccinations cause autism."

I've been through the whole second-banana scenario twice. You know what? I survived just fine.

It's true: for the first year of their life, most babies want Mommy. Especially YOU. During each infancy, Mommy would be holding either you or Sister. When I'd reach out, you (or your sister) would look at me with suspicious eyes and nuzzle deeply into her shoulder. I was chopped liver. Unknown, and unwanted.

But over time, that shifted.

It started easily enough, with the "arms up" motion from the crib. Somewhere around nine months into your respective existences, you and Sister started to figure out that Dad was an OK substitute for Mommy if she wasn't around. When confused and sad — a baby's natural waking state — they just want held. I can't give you a date, but I do remember the first time I leaned over to pick up each of you and you actually lifted your arms for me: "I want up, and you'll do."

Yes, as soon as Mommy would walk into the room you would lunge for her, but until that moment I was a warm enough body to suffice.

After age one, even more growth occurs. Somewhere around that milestone, Mommy was holding you. I walked over and held out my hands, smiling.

"Want to come to Daddy?" I asked. It had never worked before, but that doesn't mean I gave up.

As always, you looked at me questioningly. But after a second or two, you leaned forward, extending your arms. You were actively giving up being held by Mommy, for me. A "cutting onions" moment if ever one existed.

It was the same for Sister. For the first year of her life I did everything I could for her. She was a gassy little bugger, so when bubbles were upsetting her tummy I'd lay awake from 2 a.m. to 6 a.m. with her on my chest. When she was in her crib, she'd cry and cry until the gas came out. When on my chest, the instant she started to squirm I'd ever-so-gently jiggle her. She would poot, sigh, and relax. All while staying asleep. I was her hero of the overnight.

The instant she woke up? MOMMY!

I earned nothing for my efforts.

Which is fine. I wasn't supposed to. Parenting is a joy, but it's also a sacrifice. You cannot pretend you're putting effort in for the reward of being liked by an infant; you do what needs done because it needs done.

Today, Sister is officially a Daddy's Girl. When she sneaks out of her room at 3 a.m., she crawls into my side of the bed and curls up next to me. When she's upset she wants held by Daddy. That isn't to say she doesn't love Mommy, but I have become her comfort zone.

Parenting isn't a competition.

Yes, nursing creates one of the most delicate, intimate bonds that exists in life. That shouldn't be denied because men "miss out" on it.

We dads will wait our turn dutifully. If you are a loving, kind, and patient father, the baby will eventually catch up.

And it's worth it.

So. The point is: if someday you decide to enter the realm of fatherhood, do your best to find a partner that's into breastfeeding.

If you don't?

Yeah... you're going to get an earful from Mommy.

Love,

Dad

October 16

Hey Buddy…

I am in Cincinnati, and after my show last night went leafing through the book I wrote for your sister. Like you are reading now, it was a series of letters I wrote to her. Somewhere in it, I mentioned a specific, recurring nightmare I had maybe once a year.

In this nightmare, I was with my ex-girlfriend, Judy. This would cause me to wake up in a panic, wondering why we were still together.

My relationship with Judy was draining, and damaging. I'm not going to rehash everything already written elsewhere, but the long and short of it is that I loved her, and she cheated on me. That said, my time with Judy was an amazing learning opportunity. The fact I fell in love with someone who didn't love me back shaped every relationship I had from that point forward. Ultimately, it allowed me to find Mommy.

Back to the nightmare.

After each one, I'd wonder how long they'd continue. Despite being infrequent, they were annoying. Sometimes I'd get frustrated, wondering why that part of my life still lived on somewhere inside the recesses of my mind.

Only last night, after stumbling across it in Sister's book did I realize: I haven't had the nightmare since the last time I wrote about it on July 12, 2014.

Until now, that is.

It's 3:36 a.m., and I had my first Judy dream in over two years. Take note that I wrote "dream," not "nightmare."

Tonight, I didn't wake in a panic, because this time was different.

In tonight's dream, I was in Judy's apartment post-breakup, ostensibly to pick up things I had left behind. There were childhood toys I had forgotten I owned, as well as other things old and without meaning or value. These are items Judy wouldn't have had in her possession, but dreams are anything but logical. The point is: I was in her apartment, looking over my wares…

…and I realized that I just didn't want them anymore.

I was looking at each toy with confused disinterest, the very clear thought in my head: Why am I saving this? It serves no purpose in my life.

And that's when I awoke.

There was no panic, no emotions, no racing heart rate or worry. Just a sense of calm.

I believe I had the dream for two reasons: obviously reading the letter in Sister's book bubbled up old memories, but my friend Kennedy also played a hand in things.

Earlier in the day, she and I had a discussion on failed relationships. Kennedy was adamant in her belief that people need to have a final, all-cards-on-the-table conversation at the end of a relationship. I argued otherwise.

My stance led her to say, "This is a perfect example of a major difference between men and women. We tend to want closure, to understand, to talk about why everything ended. Men, not so much."

I disagree.

Men want closure — to understand why everything ended — also. But I think time and perspective is enough; sometimes you don't need to talk through anything. I don't want to fall into a gender stereotype trap — men think this way, women think that way — I think it's a people thing. Some people want to talk, while others need to reflect.

Judy never explained her actions. One day we were together, the next day she was with another man and it was over. I received no justification for what she did. It hurt at the time, but after a while the "why" became less and less important. What happened, happened. The event is set in historical stone, and there's nothing I can do about it. So why nitpick reasons?

I took a long time off to heal — two years in therapy. But it was solid, inward-looking therapy. There was no distraction from the pain, no, "If you're feeling down, I'll prescribe a pill!" There was also no denying my role in the dysfunction; I wasn't allowed to point fingers and lay the blame solely at her feet. I was asked why I chased after and remained with an emotionally-distant person for many years. I had to take accountability for my insecurities, and my desire to please another at my own expense.

Owning up to my responsibilities to both myself and a partner allowed my next relationship to occur with an emotionally giving woman. That lasted several years, and though it didn't work out, we remain friends to this day. After the infidelity, every new relationship helped teach me what to look for in a woman, and what kind of person I work best with. Dating helped me fine-tune everything to the point I eventually met Mommy.

Though it is a cliché, the truth of the matter is that Judy afforded me the ability to be happy. It's simplistic, yes, but sometimes simple is all that's needed. I don't need to have a discussion with her to find that ever-elusive closure, I've received it by way of love and family. Going back and looking for specifics would add nothing of value to my life.

To put it another way: some people want to know why something happened, others just accept that it happened.

I fall into the latter category.

It can take a long time for heartbreak to be purged from your system. Trace elements of old pain can still exist inside a healthy body and heart. But when they're gone, they're gone. And that's a good feeling.

When you're young, a failed relationship can be devastating. It can hurt like nobody's business, and leave you feeling like you'll never meet "The One." Some people carry this desperation with them until it covers them like a cloak.

Let this note remind you that no matter how much you hurt over rejection or a breakup, something better is just across the horizon. You might not be able to see it, but it's out there. All you have to do is keep moving toward it.

Promise.

Love,

Dad

October 24

Hey Buddy...

It is 11:30 p.m., and I am sitting in my recliner typing away at you.

Tonight I was at a casino only twenty minutes south of our home; you know how much I love local gigs.

(Short drive home > long drive home. Duh.)

Most people don't realize this, but comedians don't always perform in comedy clubs; we go wherever the paycheck takes us. Given that, I recently had one of the most diverse six-day spans of my career.

On Sunday, I finished a four-night run in a major American city. The room was urban, and African-Americans made up 95% (or more) of the audience.

(Point of note: our particular race is what's known as "Honkey." Or "Cracker-American," if we're being politically correct.)

On Wednesday, I performed for veteran wives in a small-town Iowa VFW hall. These weren't veterans of our most recent wars in Iraq or Afghanistan, we're talking Korea or earlier. The average age of the blue-hairs was seventy-five, at best. I have no clue how comedy was chosen over "knitting-circle" as the evening's entertainment, but it wasn't my place to wonder. My job was to provide giggles.

(Second point of note: I am a member of Generation X, and performing for The Greatest Generation is not something I do often. Most comedy shows start later than 7 p.m. , when the grandparents are asleep. I make that crack because at 6:25 p.m. I heard the organizer tell a subordinate, "OK, let's get this comedy thing going. I've gotta get home and go to bed.")

On Saturday, I opened for comedy legend Louie Anderson at a casino. This means the median age was fifty-five, or slightly less "Get off my lawn!" than at the VFW hall.

(Third point of note: Opening for a famous comedian is always a crap shoot. Will the audience pay attention to you, or will they talk amongst themselves while waiting for the main event? Bonus point of note: I found out after the fact that Louie hand-picked me for the show. A half-dozen comedians were offered, and after watching video of each, he chose me. I cannot lie, that was a boost to Dad's ego.)

Overall, I faced three disparate audiences, and was able to make them all laugh.

Comedians might be the only artists who face such a unique challenge. Jazz musicians don't get booked at rock clubs, and the entertainment director of a hospice wouldn't hire a hip-hop artist. No one would hire a carnival caricaturist to paint a family portrait, and it is doubtful you'd contract a still-life photographer to shoot your wedding. Comedians, however, are expected to be universally amusing. Even though individual members of an audience have varied tastes in food, music, clothing, and comedy, whatever comedian is on stage at the moment is expected to appeal to all of them. It's technically not fair, but to quote Omar: "It's all in the game."

(If I'm a good dad, you'll know who Omar is by the time you read this. If I've made mistakes, that last quote will leave you confused.)

There are two ways to reach an audience: One, go lowest common denominator and paint with such a wide stroke that everything is "funny." Pandering is easy, and people as a whole like easy: "Men and women are different..." "Traffic, it's crazy!" Things that are tried (and tired) and true can get people laughing every time.

The second option is to pinpoint what you do, to go to the core of who you are and make your act so personal everyone connects with you, even if they don't always relate to the material. You might lose one or two people, but you should be able to win an overwhelming majority.

I prefer the second path. By telling personal stories, I am able to share my enthusiasm with the audience and take them on a ride. This means that in an urban room, a white guy like me can do material about being a father that any parent can enjoy.

When being personal, you try and make your jokes so funny that relating to them doesn't matter. One of the best compliments I've ever received is when a Millennial told me, "Dude, when you were talking about your kids, I was laughing my ass off, and I don't even have kids." Even though the topic wasn't personal to him, I was able to make my experiences universal.

Is that all there is to it? Almost.

With comedy, everything breaks down into content, appearance, and delivery. Someone with great content, yet horrible delivery, can fail. Conversely, someone with horrible content and fantastic delivery can succeed. Typically, African-American audiences are interested in delivery. Many African-American comics — Kat

Williams and Bernie Mac, for example—have said, "It's about appearance and attitude." You have to show confidence and take command of the room. If you're on stage, you have to show you deserve to be up there and hit with jokes quickly. In all honesty, my first show in the urban room wasn't the best. I didn't strike out, but I didn't hit it out of the park. I had to get a feel for things, and once I found my footing everything went great.

White audiences can be a little more patient, giving you more time to set things up. They still want the payoff, but you can tell stories with the funny sprinkled in as opposed to rapid fire. Interesting works almost as well as funny. At the VFW hall, I basically talked to the women. I still told jokes, but everything was more conversational than it otherwise might have been.

(Older audiences also prefer cleaner material. You can drop some innuendo, as long as it's playful and not blatant; hint at being naughty, without being dirty. You'd also do best to lose the four-letter words.)

Regarding appearance, the simple fact of the matter is that people judge other people. It happens unconsciously, and automatically. If you're on stage in a T-shirt and torn jeans, a VFW hall of elderly women or theater full of adults might not respond as quickly as they would someone dressed crisply. (For that matter, a group of college kids might view a comedian wearing a suit as stiff and unapproachable. Which isn't to say you cannot win over an audience despite your appearance, but snap judgments are made as you're walking to the stage.)

You can't please everyone, however. No matter what you try, someone probably won't enjoy your act. Sometimes they were just looking for something else; sometimes they just don't like you.

At the VFW hall, one elderly woman went out of her way to tell me of her displeasure with the entertainment. She approached with a huff, stating: "You comics were too political. That one," she intoned while pointing at my opening act, "made fun of Trump!"

When I asked her what was wrong with that, she barked, "Comedians shouldn't talk politics! You should make different jokes!"

I asked what kind of jokes she was interested in and the now near-apoplectic woman shouted, "I don't know! Maybe 'Why did the chicken cross the road?' That's what Bob Hope did!"

Comedians usually have a sure-fire response for whatever is tossed their way; they're used to being heckled and badgered by the audience. It's been several days, and I still don't have a clever retort for that one. To me, it was as bewildering as someone suggesting the Great Pyramids of Egypt were used for grain storage.

(And who would ever say something that stupid?)

Anyway, no matter what situation you're in—save for a fraternity, ugh, please don't join one of those Goddamn things— you will come across a multitude of opinions during your life. You will walk among myriad religions, sexual orientations, genders, races, and wander through many regions of the country, if not world.

Don't fear these people, embrace them. Be yourself, and understand that we are all different on this rock called Earth. Don't sell out and change for others, but adapt and understand how to remain uniquely you in a situation where you might be outnumbered by "other."

Or, to quote Sting: Be yourself, no matter what they say…

(Bet you thought I was going to go with Shakespeare there. Nope, too easy a pull.)

Love,

Dad

October 29

Hey Buddy…

I am not a bright person.

So if there are two people on my Facebook (Google it, if that reference is outdated by the time you read this) friend list with nearly identical names — and by that I mean same first names and oh-so-similar last names — it would be easy to assume I would confuse the two.

Especially when, and this is important, one of them uses a kitten as their profile picture.

The other month, a woman popped up in my "Hey, it's your friend's birthday!" feed. Using only a glance, I figured it was the fitness instructor whose classes I like to attend. As one might expect of a fitness instructor, she's in superb shape from top to bottom, with rips and cuts and curves aplenty to flaunt. It was Wednesday, her day to teach Body Attack, so I scribbled a little ditty on her wall: "Happy Birthday! In honor of your special day, I'm skipping the gym tonight and going out to eat pizza and get fat, just for you!"

Get it? It's a joke; she's a fitness instructor, and I was going to skip her class to eat unhealthy food! Ha-ha! It's like being clever, only not.

Anyway, a few weeks later I received another notice for my fitness instructor friend from that lovely birthday monitoring service, Facebook. Confused, I went to her wall and wrote,

"Didn't I just wish you a happy birthday? Geez, how many do you need a year?"

And that was that.

For about an hour.

Until my mind started putting together the pieces of the puzzle, and I decided to go scroll down her profile wall.

My "pizza and get fat" comment was nowhere to be found, so... where was it?

Turns out, I had left the comment on another woman's wall, one whose name is two letters different from the fitness instructor. A woman who was, as chance would have it, a little larger than your average woman, but probably right in line with a legal resident of Mississippi.

That's right, I went to the profile of a woman who was overweight and told her I was going to get fat in her honor.

Yup. Open mouth, insert foot.

Well, I suppose that's what people get when they use cats instead of personal pictures to represent themselves.

Anyway, I am in Des Moines, staying at Graw Diane's house and performing at the local comedy club. Mommy will bring you, Sister, and Kitty over this weekend. I can't wait to see all of you.

Love,

Dad

November 18

Hey Buddy...

I am in the tiny town of Windom, Minnesota.

Before my show, I was farting around online, and I came across an article posted by a friend: 5 Reasons Marriage Doesn't Work Anymore. Her "YES!" indicated she enthusiastically agreed with the author. That author, for the record, was a relationship advice columnist. He was an expert since he was in his twenties and had been married three whole years before getting divorced.

Like anyone susceptible to click-bait, I gave the piece a gander. Within a few moments, I was rolling my eyes and frustrated. Frustrated by the author's trite nonsense, and let down by society at large for sharing it and treating the words as truth.

The commentary was a litany of whining, excuses, and superficiality. Your sex life fades. People spend too much time on their phones. Social media makes people selfish. Everything is too expensive these days, crippling couples financially.

There was one item of importance missing from the list: personal responsibility. The main reason a marriage falls apart is because the couple doesn't put in the effort.

Marriage is work. Hard. Work.

That giddy feeling you feel during the infancy of the relationship goes away. It can be replaced by either a deep bond, or apathy. If you think you're going to look at your partner ten years deep and feel the same way you did the first time you saw them, you're delusional.

The immature or shallow chase butterflies, forever jumping from partner to partner celebrating the newness of each relationship and being confused and scared when those butterflies leave their belly. Those ready for commitment and challenge, willing to put in a little blood, sweat, and tears? They will make their marriages last. Marriage isn't winning the lottery; the jackpot is finding that someone willing to put in the effort with you, like I have found with your mother.

It wasn't easy getting here; we both went through several unsuccessful relationships before figuring out what we both wanted, and more importantly needed, in a partner. Failure is what you make of it. You can let it beat you down and be defeatist, or learn and grow from it.

From what I read in the "marriage doesn't work" article, the author learned nothing. I wonder why. Maybe he's not self-reflective enough; maybe he didn't have a good mentor.

Either way, it is my duty to help you understand relationships.

You will learn the most by watching Mom and I interact. Parents are the key to any relationship their children have. But I'd like to do more, and go after the article (even though you haven't read it) with a point-by-point response.

First, the author complained about sex, and the absence of it. His marriage was without passion or spontaneity. Look, you're not going to like reading this, but the disgusting truth is: Mom and I have sex. So there. Yes, gross, whatever. Keep reading.

Is the sex we share the same as the first few months we were together? No. We have it less often, and it's more scheduled than spur-of-the-moment. But the physical and emotional attraction is still there, and that's what's important. We make time for what we do; it doesn't have to be impulsive.

Next came the argument that marriage is generational, and that times are different today than they were for our grandparents. Which is good and all, if the author didn't also say his generation was crippled by college tuition and home mortgages. The juxtaposing thoughts were written without any sense of irony or hypocrisy. My grandparents lived through the freaking Great Depression. Which situation is worse: an expensive house you have to pay for, or soup kitchen lines that extend around a city block? If someone can't figure that out on their own, opening their eyes is an impossible task.

Next up, technology: "You text your partner instead of talking to them. You use an app to buy flowers instead of..." what, calling and ordering them? (Using the phone would be considered technology, too.) Well, if you don't like technology, set it aside a little while every day. Mom makes it a point to have face-to-face discussions before bed. You and Sister are asleep, the TV is off, our phones put away. Even if it's only for five minutes, we're talking to one another. More importantly, we're listening to one another. Communication drives a marriage, and you know what? I don't see anything wrong with texting. Mom and I message constantly, from little nothings to jolts of love in the form of pictures of you and Sister. Technology is not a burden, it's a blessing. Anyone that feels otherwise can convert to the Amish way of life and move to Pennsylvania Dutch Country. Maybe that will save their next marriage.

Another complaint was social media. "Nothing is private; everything gets posted online." By the time I got to that one, I was legitimately angry, because nothing gets posted if you choose not to post it. People don't get to whine "everything is online," because posting on social media is not mandatory. You don't have to take pictures of your every meal, you don't have to own a selfie stick, and if a tree falls in a forest and no one live-tweets it, guess what? The tree still fell.

And if looking at other, "happier" couples online makes you insecure? Then don't look at other couples.

("Social media" as an excuse was combined with a shaken-fist attitude toward our self-centered ways, but that issue is a non-starter. People have been self-absorbed since the dawn of time. To say narcissism caused a marriage to fail means you married the wrong person, or that you've got issues of your own to work out.)

Look, there are legitimate reasons a marriage might not succeed. When the effort outweighs the rewards, a relationship isn't worth saving. Sometimes you drift away from your partner. But that happens over the course of many years, not three.

I have a couple of decades-old friends who are shadows of their former selves; I barely know who they are anymore, so I can only imagine how their spouses feel. I also know one legitimate sociopath who fools people up front, only to expose himself slowly over time.

(Shocker: he's on his third marriage. Start your egg timers.)

Struggling through infertility will put a strain on any couple, and hell, so will infidelity. If someone can't be faithful, the partnership should be terminated. And God… a domestic abuse situation. That shouldn't even be a question.

So, yeah. Some marriages won't last. But if your marriage failed "because Facebook made me sad," then you're just blathering on. Maybe take a good long look in the mirror instead. Things change, people change, hairstyles change, and interest rates fluctuate. Change with them, but don't blame them for your failings.

(Sorry about that. Things just got a little angry. I was upset with the author of the silly/stupid article I read, not you.)

What I'm trying to say is that you are responsible for your own life and actions.

Very little in life is easy. Marriage is hard. You have to work at it like you work at anything. I don't want you to end up like the author of the article, someone pointing fingers and laying blame for his failures on others. I want you to be self-reliant, and reflective. When something doesn't go your way, be it a relationship or otherwise, I want you to square your shoulders, contemplate what happened and your role in it, and move on.

Be strong.

I love you.

Dad

December 5

Hey Buddy...

I am in Fargo, North Dakota.

This morning I went out in search of a diner to grab a bite to eat. While there, I spotted an elderly couple having coffee, holding hands over the table. I cannot say I know what the secret to a lasting relationship is—compromise, communication, or the like—I do know this: whenever I see an elderly couple holding hands, I think, someday, that will be Lydia and me.

Love,

Dad

December 11

Hey Buddy...

I'm working the local comedy club this weekend, which means I get to return home every night after work. Close-to-home gigs are my favorite for this very reason. I always drive home after my shows, but when the trip is twenty minutes versus twelve hours? That's quite the treat.

The long commutes, by the way, are why most Sunday mornings you and Sister find me in the guest bedroom in the basement. When I drive overnight after those gigs, I'm completely wiped out. What happens is: I'll wake up on Saturday around 7 a.m. at the latest, be awake all day, go perform my shows, then hop in the car and get home anywhere between 3 a.m. and 8 a.m. More often than not, I'll be awake 24 hours solid by the time my head hits the pillow.

That being the case, I'll steal away downstairs to get at least a couple of hours of snoozing in before Mommy tells you and Sister, "If you go to the basement, there's a surprise waiting for you..."

It's worth it to be sleep deprived, though. I'd rather have the two of you wake me up after a two-hour snooze than drive all day Sunday and miss one of the only full days we have together as a family.

As far as other sleeping habits go, during the week you generally stumble out of your bedroom in the morning and discover me on the couch. I don't know why it's important for me to address this, but I feel compelled to nonetheless.

When I was a teenager, my parents slept in separate bedrooms. They said it was because they kept different schedules, but I suspected it was because they were growing tired of the charade that was their marriage—their divorce a few years later would prove me right.

When you find me on the couch, you climb up on me and snuggle in, and after a few moments determine that you "want squares," which is your description of Life cereal. Circles, naturally, are Cheerios. I've no clue what Rice Krispies are, as you eat them so infrequently.

Up and to your high chair we away, and I retrieve your cereal. We eat together, smiling at one another and in many ways reenacting a famous scene from the movie Jaws. In it, a father and son mimic one another, and that's what you and I do in our quiet, morning moments. You smile wide, so I smile wide. You take one hand and open-palm your head, and I mirror you. This continues with a bevy of facial movements and bodily gestures, until you are no longer eating and instead giggling furiously.

It's quite heartwarming.

Getting back to the meat of the matter: you find me on the couch because I do not sleep well. Sadly, I think you have inherited this condition of mine; you fall asleep with difficulty and wake easily. It might be something you have to learn to live with.

I try to be productive in the wee hours of the night. I used to wake up at 3 a.m. and just stare at the ceiling, wishing I could fall back asleep and wondering why I was awake. Now, if I wake up and realize I'm going to be awake for a while, I get up and write. I hop on the computer and type away, sometimes editing these letters, sometimes working on jokes, and eventually I get so tired I just decide to close my computer and fall asleep right there.

The other reason you find me on the couch is because I'm an oven in bed.

I'll go to bed with Mommy in our room, and four or five hours later wake up hot, hot, hot. Even if I'm not sleeping under any covers, I've still turned the mattress into a heating pad. It's absorbed so much of my body heat that it's uncomfortable (and impossible) to sleep on.

So, I head out to the couch, which is cool to the touch. At first, at least. There have been some nights where I start and finish the night in what you and Sister call "Mommy/Daddy bedroom." If the couch gets too hot (because I've been there so long), I'll steal back to bed and finish my almost-slumber there.

Either way, I love you, Sister, and Mommy. And yes, Kitty and even Simon. Sometimes.

Which means I don't want you to think that me sleeping all over the house is a sign of unhappiness. I just happen to be the world's worst sleeper. And despite the current evidence, I hope you haven't inherited my condition.

Love,

Dad

December 19

Hey Buddy…

I am in Stillwater, Oklahoma.

I have read that no matter how old children get, parents always view them through the lens of nostalgia. Even when the children are full-grown adults, parents see the wobbly toddlers they raised.

As of this writing, you are one, plus a couple of months in spare change. Mommy and I take turns reading to you nightly; your favorite book is Clifford's Animal Sounds. We read it, set it on the end table, and you lean over, pick it back up, and return it to us. If we lacked resolve, you would have us page through it a hundred times in a row.

A simple book, the sentences are short and sweet. Perfect for a one-year-old. "The cat says meow." "The hen says cluck," that sort of thing.

Because she loves interaction, Mommy began reading each passage, then asking you to repeat it. She reads, "The cat says meow," and then asks, "What does the cat say?" You, no matter what the animal, give the same response. You gaze at us with a mix of confidence and pleasure, smile with your mouth shut, and offer a double grunt.

"What does the cat say?"

Grunt-grunt.

"What does the cow say?"

Grunt-grunt.

You do this for every animal but one.

When asked, "What does the sheep say?" you light up like a Christmas tree. Your eyes go wide, and your normal mouth-shut smile becomes a full-face, mouth-open-wide joyful bellow as you intone "BAAAAAAAAA."

Your petite head shakes from side to side as you drag the sound out, and you lean toward us ever so slightly. I can tell you're proud of yourself because you know you are imitating this animal correctly.

(And because you are basking in the love you see in our eyes and hear in our laughter as we react).

The image of you shaking your head, "Baaaa" exiting your little lungs... that was all I had in my head the other night while watching a movie called *Star Wars: The Force Awakens*. In it, a character named Ben Solo killed his father, Han. The look on Han's face as it happened wasn't shock or anger, but sorrow. The way Han caressed Ben's face one final time before falling into the abyss was heartbreaking.

I wondered what was going through Han's head at that moment. Was it something from Ben's infancy? Something so tender to him, an instant forever etched in his mind that he saw whenever he looked at Ben? Or maybe Han felt remorse, believing it was his failings as a father that allowed them to become so estranged.

Of all the things I took away from *The Force Awakens*, the most prevalent was wanting to be a better father. The movie is a sci-fi fantasy with laser guns and light sabers, yes, but I still left the theater imagining all the parenting missteps that could put you on a path to drug addiction, dropping out of school, suicide — all the "dark sides" of real life.

I wonder how the bonds between parent and child sever. Does it happen gradually, over time, or through one climatic event? No parent sets out to disappoint, but it happens all too often. Your career makes demands, or you want to maintain a semblance of your old life and hang out with friends like you used to. Somewhere along the way you neglect your child. Maybe you don't mean to be, but you're always "busy" when they need help. Maybe they always see your nose buried in your phone and "learn their place" unconsciously. Maybe they fall in with the wrong crowd at school.

I'm still a relatively new father; in no way do I know what I'm doing. Parenting is trial and error at best, but some things seem like common sense, little nothings that can (hopefully) keep a child on the right path. Smiling when you make eye contact. Being genuinely enthused spending time with you. Having discussions with you, not wagging a finger and saying "No!" without explanation. Then again, I could easily do everything "right" and everything will still go wrong, because life happens.

Movies are supposed to make us feel something. Comedies make us laugh, horror films frighten us... I'm not sure a spaghetti western set in space was supposed to make me wax philosophic on fatherhood, but it did.

Hopefully it nudged me in the right direction.

Hopefully I'll be a good father to you.

Love,

Dad

January 2

Hey Buddy…

"Orv is all gone."

Sister said those words in her typical sing-song manner as we drove by Orv's house. She was neither sad, nor happy, just straightforward. Orv had died one day earlier.

He was 95, so his passing wasn't a surprise. In fact, the day before, Mommy had stopped by his house to say her goodbyes. I had noticed an inordinate number of cars parked around his home, and by that I mean literally around his home. They filled his driveway, were on his front and side lawn...

It was an ominous sign.

I shot Mommy a text telling her she should probably visit, which she did. The house was filled with the tears of many family and friends. Orv was bedridden.

The friendship between Mommy and Orv was accidental and organic. Orv's house sat on the corner of a busy four-way stop in town, and all summer long motorists could see him on his porch, taking in the world and smiling at anyone who tossed a wave his way.

Mommy and I would pass Orv's house either while driving or walking Kitty. Over time, she decided to approach the man to whom she was continually raising her hand. Orv was 92 at the time, and a widower. He lived alone and loved visitors. Mommy stopped that first time while pregnant with Sister, eventually introducing him to her, and later you as the years passed.

Orv had his ups and downs; we visited him in a nursing home once, where he was spending several weeks recuperating from a bad fall. He lost his driver's license after riding up on the curb and hitting a sign... not that such a minor accident stopped Orv from completing his coffee run that morning. He just climbed down out of his pickup truck, left it where it was, and walked the final block to McDonald's.

"I figured the cops would find me if they needed me," he explained matter-of-factly.

Even with instances like those under his belt, Orv was still independent enough to remain under his own roof. Orv was not one for the likes of a retirement home.

After her deathbed visit, Mommy returned home in tears. Confused, Sister asked why she was sad, and we explained as best we could that Orv was dying.

Death is difficult enough for adults to come to terms with, but children just don't get it; death is too abstract a concept.

Which is where Disney comes into play.

Disney loves death, and they constantly use it as a plot point in their films. From Big Hero 6 to Finding Nemo, and dating all the way back to the original heartbreak movie, Bambi, death is at the center of many Disney stories.

("Mother, where are you?")

Using scenes from Sister's favorite movies, Mommy and I were able to explain that Orv was "gone," like Tadashi in Big Hero 6.

68

Tadashi went into the building, and it blew up. Orv... well, he didn't blow up, he had just reached his time; his body stopped working. Two different ways of going, but each with the same outcome.

(We wanted to avoid saying Orv died in his sleep, or that he got sick. Children latch on to certain bits of information differently than we'd like them to, and we didn't need Sister fearing either illness or going to sleep. "What if I don't wake up?" opens a whole new can of worms.)

It's been several months, now. As we drive by Orv's old house, a "For Rent" sign firmly placed in the front yard, Sister still alternately states, "Orv gone" confidently, or asks, "When Orv coming back? When him is all done being dead, him will be back tomorrow?"

She's not sad, just inquisitive. We continually point out that after he died, Tadashi wasn't in the movie anymore. Unfortunately, that means Orv won't return to the movie called life.

Disney has been a helpful bridge for our discussions on death, so kudos to them for singing its melody in so many movies. When parenting gets tough, Disney creates a great starting point for what is normally a difficult conversation.

They broach the subject with such brutal honesty that when Sister watches Finding Nemo these days, after the barracuda attack she says quite ably, "Coral is dead."

And then she enjoys the rest of the movie, completely unaware she's dealt with the subject more gracefully than adults ever can.

Someday you'll have to learn what death is, too.

Fortunately, Mommy and I have both Sister, and Disney, to help us when that time comes.

Love,

Dad

January 8

Hey Buddy...

I've been through a couple of less-than-stellar breakups in my lifetime.

I'm sure I've already written several letters about them, and will probably bore you with several more, but that's not entirely what this note is about, so stick with me.

One relationship occurred with a regular customer at a club where I used to perform. At the end, as she was dumping me, I told her: "This isn't going to be fun for me, so please, one favor? Don't contact me."

Since I wasn't in control of the breakup, I wanted to maintain some semblance of power over what was happening in my life. I wanted the separation to be as permanent as possible. Carrying on as friends wasn't a viable option. Unfortunately, she didn't agree, and would call me randomly.

She didn't want to get back together, probably, but she wasn't 100% positive, how was I doing, no, we shouldn't get back together, maybe, but she just wanted to talk to me, to hear my voice...

It exhausted me.

By the time I was slated to return to her city, things were fairly strained between us. I had been alternately ignoring and taking her calls, and I felt like a yo-yo tied to her whims. The week before my arrival, I sent what I thought was a respectful little email: "Hey, I don't know if you know this, but I'm coming to town, and I know you like hanging out at the club, but it would mean a lot to me if for just this one weekend you wouldn't. If I could be allowed to just slip in and out without having to deal with the emotions of the breakup, it would be a lot easier on me. Thanks."

Naturally, she not only showed up, but did so with her new boyfriend in tow. Her attitude, as she later explained, was, "Hey, I hang out here and shouldn't have to stay away just because you can't deal with it."

I avoided her, went about my business, and that was that.

A week later, however, she blogged about what a jerk I was, and how she was above the petty emotions I had. Her actions and words struck me as unnecessarily cruel, and it was exactly what I needed to finally be over her.

Years passed, and I attended the wedding of one of my oldest friends. At one point while we visited, my friend asked about my ex. At that moment, surrounded by joyous people celebrating love and union, I had that alcoholic's moment of clarity—danke, Pulp Fiction. I decided I didn't want any bad blood in my past and that I should reach out to her. I didn't want to be friends, or even be casual acquaintances, but I did feel that since things had ended somewhat sloppily, the mess could be tidied up.

Riding the high of my good mood, I sent an email stating: "I'm sure there were points in the breakup where I acted poorly, and I'm sorry for any behavior of mine that may have been perceived as hurtful."

The response I got was, "Apology accepted." It came with a smiley face.

While I didn't think I had been apologizing to hear it in return, I immediately realized that was indeed the case. I had expressed regret for my actions not because I believed I had done her any wrong, but because I assumed that opening a dialogue might pave the way to a better closing note than had previously sounded. When that moment didn't arrive—when she didn't apologize for ignoring my wishes and flaunting her current boy-toy in front of me—I was...

...well, to be honest, I don't know how I felt.

I wasn't hurt or angry. I wasn't really surprised, either. If anything, it made sense. I had acted with selfish intent; my words were a wolf in sheep's clothing. Though an apology, my email was an attempt to trick her into asking forgiveness. My actions were entirely inappropriate, because apology should come from a point of genuine remorse. That way, if it's not reciprocated, no offense is taken.

I make that last statement, because it is one of the most natural of human exchanges; if two people have a disagreement or a spat, one will eventually say, "I'm sorry," causing the other to respond in kind, "I'm sorry, too." When the second person forgoes that responsibility, it leaves the first person hanging.

We've all been there.

Anyway, because of that lesson, I went into future situations with better intentions. Case in point: a friend and I got into a row and stopped talking to one another. Though his hand in the matter was almost as tainted as mine, I knew I had done wrong by him. I felt manning up and apologizing was the right thing to do, and did so. I don't know if he mulled it over, but eventually we began speaking again and remained friends.

The thing is, he never apologized for his part in the disagreement; I never got an "I'm sorry, too."

I've always remembered that fact. It doesn't weigh on me, but I haven't forgotten it. Having had the experience with my ex, when I apologized to my friend I wasn't looking for a response. Had he given one, it would have been nice, but he didn't, and that's that. I did what I thought was right and could now exist with a clear conscience.

(Of course, the probability exists that he sleeps fine at night, too, feeling justified in his inaction. Character flaws wear many faces.)

So, what is the point of my rambling?

I guess it's the idea that apology is about absolution, and amends. You apologize because it relieves an ache in your soul, or because it is the honorable action. Never apologize to hear the phrase repeated your way. I could have just written that, I suppose, but it would have been out of context, and left me with nothing to do while trapped inside this hotel room.

A hotel room, for the record, in Bay Mills, Michigan.

Love,

Dad

January 16

Hey Buddy...

I am in Fairview Heights, Illinois, and right now, I suspect a mother is out there talking about me.

I say that, because I am about to talk about her.

Two days ago, I was at a play area with you and Sister. One of those enclosed, foam-object/spongy-floored deals, where you can fall and bounce to your heart's delight. On this particular day, it was relatively crowded. People wanted to get out of the house, but winter chills kept us all from partaking in outside activities.

Sister was running around; you were climbing all over me. We had been in the room ten minutes, everyone playing amicably, when I heard Sister forcefully shouting, "No! I don't like that!"

I looked up to see her yelling at a boy a little above her age. Sister had her scolding face on, something she wears when irritated by you, Kitty, or an inanimate object that won't bend to her will. The two children were about four feet apart, and he was roaring at her playfully. I'm not sure if he was pretending to be a lion, dinosaur, or some other beast, but he was happily yelling "RAWR!" every few moments, albeit through a smile. Each time he did, Sister wagged a finger: "You stop!"

I giggled a bit, but I also noticed a furrowed-brow mom watching the situation.

After a couple more seconds of the "RAWR!"/"I don't like that!" back and forth, the woman intervened.

"Simon, you need to listen to her. Stop that," she gently scolded.

The boy moved on, defeated.

I thought the moment odd. From what I saw, they were kids being kids. Neither one was really bullying the other, and nothing violent was happening; they were working things out on their own. Learning social skills, so to speak.

A little while later, Sister was by me, climbing a toy frog. The "RAWR" boy wandered over and started climbing next to her. Because it was a smallish toy, he eventually bumped into Sister. Not hard, not on purpose, just two people trying to fit into a tiny space. Like commuters on a Japanese subway.

The mom jumped up, bee-lined over, picked up her son, and took him away with another scolding: "That little girl was playing there first!"

Again, I cocked my head like a puzzled puppy. The kids were doing their best to figure out how to play in the same area at the same time. From what I saw, they were learning how to interact with one another. Granted, maybe the mom knew something I didn't; maybe her son had a temper and threw tantrums at the drop of a hat, but it didn't feel like that. It felt like worry — what will other parents think of me if my son misbehaves? — and control.

As said, she may be telling someone about me at this very moment. "His daughter was yelling at Simon, and he didn't do anything!"

76

Fair enough. But I did nothing, because I thought no action was warranted. Had Sister and her son become physical — shoving or hitting — I would have jumped in. But sometimes you have to sit back and let kids explore solutions to their own problems. The boy wanted to roar; Sister didn't like it. Big whoop. He'll eventually understand not everyone likes his noise, and she'll have to learn that the whole world doesn't fall to their knees at her command.

Plus, and maybe I'm giving this too much thought, I'm raising a daughter here. I want to empower her. If she's willing to stand her ground against a boy bigger than her, why would I want to knock that out of her system? If I begin a system of shutting her down and stepping in to help at every stage, there's a chance she'll become infused with either self-doubt or a sense of helplessness. I want her to grow into herself, and I want that person to be a confident woman someday.

(I shudder to imagine what kind of emasculated boy that woman is raising. Oh, and for the record, I won't helicopter you.)

I will say this: though I disagree with the mom on jumping in constantly to intervene, at least she was involved. Like me, she was on the floor, playing with her youngest child and being proactive when it came to her oldest.

I'll take that over the parents who bury their noses into phones the instant they sit down, oblivious to the world and the children playing around them.

Either way, there will be times you might expect me to jump in and solve a problem for you, and I won't. When things get rough, I will always be there for both you and Sister. But I'm also going to let you problem-solve on your own.

You might not like it in the moment, but I guarantee you'll appreciate it later in life.

Love,

Dad

January 23

Hey Buddy…

I am in Green Bay, Wisconsin. Last night I was in a small town in the Upper Peninsula of Michigan; tonight I will perform, then drive to Graw Janet's house. Tomorrow I will be home with you, and Mommy and Sister.

Months ago, Mommy was listening to an interview with an actor named Jason Bateman. If I've raised you correctly, you'll know who he is, because we will have binge-watched the show Arrested Development together.

As Mommy listened, one question caught her ear: "Would you let your children get into acting?"

Mommy stopped what she was doing and paid full attention to the words exiting Jason's mouth. "I wouldn't, only because it is a profession that you can't really help yourself in. In most professions, if you stay at the office an extra four hours every day, you're gonna impress the boss, you're gonna get that promotion, you're gonna get that raise, you're gonna at least have job security. But with acting, if you're really ambitious and you have a good work ethic, and are really good at your job, it might not really matter."

Mommy got lost in thought a moment, and in a very unfortunate parallel related those words to comedy, and my career. There is something odd—some might say unfair—about the artistic world, where how good you are matters much less than how lucky you are.

Which brings me to something semi-related. I cannot remember where I read this, but someone once asked a member of the Dukakis presidential campaign, "When did you realize it was over?"

The answer was surprising: "When they announced we lost."

They didn't admit defeat one month, one week, or one day out from the election. Even though the world at large knew Bush Sr. was a lock, the Dukakis people lived in such a bubble they used faith to carry them to the bitter end. That wasn't unique to the Dukakis campaign; Mitt Romney was so convinced he was going to win he didn't have a concession speech written.

Delusion isn't isolated to politics; every year on a talent show called American Idol, confident teens would declare, "I am the next American Idol!"

They'd say it full of belief, even though at the end of it all there was but one Highlander standing in victory.

So.

At what point are you supposed to become self-aware enough to understand: it's not happening?

I have been a fan of a man named David Letterman since his first Late Night.

I always wanted to meet him, to be a guest on his program. This goes back to 1982, when he premiered on NBC. I was a kid, and had absolutely no reason to be on television, but I still wanted to sit on a chair next to Dave and just… be there. Dave was cool, and I wanted to be cool by proximity.

When I decided to become a comedian, Letterman became my goal. I never had any dreams of getting my own sitcom or becoming a movie star; I just wanted to perform on Letterman's stage.

David Letterman retired on May 20, 2015.

When he ended his run, I didn't really feel anything. My biggest goal, the one dream I had always had... it was no more, and I was OK with it. Life has a way of re-calibrating your goals and what you find important. You have to roll with the punches, or you end up staring at a mirror and find Dorian Gray staring back at you.

Today, I would still do just about anything possible to get on television, but only because of the boost it would give my career. Being a good father—that has superseded any ego-based career goals I may have once had.

Unfortunately, being a good father means providing, and it is easier to provide if people know who you are. In my business, you can be the funniest, most original comic out there, but if you haven't been on TV, no one cares.

These days, the very concept of grabbing a television slot looks grim, depending on the day and my attitude. On some days, I am a blind member of the Dukakis presidential team, optimistic and full of commitment to the cause. On others days, my faith is not so strong.

Comedy is a struggle—any artistic pursuit is. It beats you up daily. There is a huge chasm between the joy of the stage and the struggle of the business. By way of example, I auditioned for a club two years ago. I heard they were looking for new faces, so I went and tried out. I did very well—better than many of the people I saw auditioning that night.

As I write to you tonight, I have not been hired there.

Meanwhile, another comedian went up that night and tanked. Their material wasn't very good, and the audience wasn't laughing. Naturally, that person works there regularly. Even worse for my ego, I spent a weekend with this comedian several years ago. They were my opening act and struggled through every show. There were a few smiles, maybe even a laugh now and then, but for a majority of the 30 minutes the comedian was on stage, there was silence.

That person has a manager, a full calendar, and was on national television last month.

You cannot make sense of these things; to try would be insane. I also don't like giving voice to these thoughts. Negativity breeds negativity, no one likes a whiner, the power of positive thinking and all that jazz...

...but I admit that sometimes I feel like Crash Davis.

Maybe it doesn't matter if I'm delusional. Maybe life is about being Rocky Balboa in the first movie, holding your ground to the bitter end and winning the moral victory while losing the fight. Maybe it's enough to know that if you try to be everything to everyone, you won't be anything to anyone. Maybe these are thoughts I try to convince myself are truths.

Maybe trying to prove Jason Bateman wrong will be my Sisyphean task.

I do know that while I cannot tell you what you can and cannot do with your life, when I hear the question, "Do you think your son will be a comedian?"

I answer with a resounding, "No."

Of course, I have no real say in your future plans. The best I can do is give advice and let you be your own person. But I hope you follow a career path with more sound footing, something with raises and bonuses that aren't tied to rubbing elbows.

Accountants may be boring, but people will always need them. More importantly, if you're good at what you do in a field like that, you have a greater shot at advancement.

Love,

Dad

January 30

Hey Buddy...

On Monday, you went to daycare on your own; Sister stayed home.

She wasn't technically sick, but you can't go to daycare within 24-hours of having a fever over 101 degrees, and on Sunday she peaked at 102. She had actually been carrying the fever for several days by then, so I made an appointment with her pediatrician to make sure we weren't dealing with an infection or anything worse.

Sister and I started our morning with a trip to the craft store for Mommy. As we drove, we listened to "Airplane Song" — Upside Down & Inside Out, by OK Go (which you and Sister both call "Color Band") — on repeat. Like most children, you both fixate on one thing, and with this particular song she loves and beats it to death. In our travels, we have probably listened to Hello! (which you and sister call "¡Hola!") from The Book of Mormon 4,657 times, and Timebomb by the Royal Crescent Mob 2,812 times. Since it's not Bieber or anything awful, the repetition doesn't bother me as much as it could.

(Not for nothing, explaining the difference to you between Timebomb by the RCM and Time Bomb by Rancid took some doing, but I think we got it figured out.)

Anyway, at the craft store, Sister discovered a sparkly hula hoop and her eyes grew wide. It was only $5, so I figured "Why not?" Little things make little ones quite happy, after all.

From there, it was off to the doctor, where we sat and colored in the waiting room, and then sat and colored in the exam room. The doctor looked at Sister's ears, eyes, nose and throat, ultimately giving her a thumbs up, but warning, "If she goes above 101 again, give us a call." People who promote wellness grow suspicious of fevers lasting as long as hers had.

(She was down to 99 degrees, according to the nurse.)

Being a man who believes in bribery, I had made a pre-visit offer: "Do well at the doctor, and we can stop at the cupcake store on the way home."

I was corrected immediately: "I don't want to stop at the cupcake store, I want to stop at the cupcake place."

Ah, yes. The cupcake place. How could I have been so dense?

Once home, we ate lunch, then watched an episode of "Abby School," which is what Sister calls Sesame Street. She's all about role models, and is drawn to characters matching her gender as opposed to "Ew, boys." Abby School may only be one segment on Sesame Street, but in her mind it is the sole reason for tuning in.

(For the record, you call Sesame Street "Elmo!")

Then, it was nap time. Which is like Hammer time, only with more napping and less parachute pants.

(You'll get that someday.)

I was exhausted, and ready for a little respite from the action. Sister had other ideas.

"Read me a book!" she shouted gleefully.

86

A simple request, yes. But as said, I was tired.

"Just go to sleep, sweetie," I sighed, attempting to exit the room.

In a span of .035 seconds, she went into full meltdown mode. I had missed her nap window by about 15 minutes, and sometimes that's all it takes. She began sobbing and crying as if I had just broken the news of her third-world-style, pre-arranged marriage to a 50-year-old goat herder.

"Read... me... a... book..." she cried, sobbing between each word.

I grew slightly exasperated, informing her while rubbing my eyes, "We read books at bedtime, not naptime."

Her howls increased; her tears flowed like Victoria Falls.

There was flailing, me explaining that crying does not mean you get your way...

...but after five minutes, I relented. It wasn't worth it, the battle of wills, or listening to her moan despondently.

I climbed into bed, and she snuggled up against me, her tears slowing as she struggled to catch her breath.

After I finished reading, I kissed her on the forehead and was halfway out of the door when she spoke up again. The timing couldn't have been more perfect; it was as if she had timed it under direction for a play or movie, something done for maximum effect when tugging heartstrings.

As I was about to close the door, she choked out a call one last time, "Daddy?"

"Yes sweetie?" I paused.

"Thank you for reading the book."

And with that, she rolled over and closed her eyes.

I stood there feeling like a complete shitheel.

Why had I let her meltdown, allowing her to cry and lose control of her emotions instead of just reading the book in the first place? Was I trying to be a firm-hand parent? Saying no for the sake of no, so she would learn she doesn't always get her way or what she wants? I don't know, but I felt awful the entire time she slept.

There are battles you face with your kids, such as "No, you can't watch whatever you want," "No, you can't eat whatever you want," and "Yes, there is a set bedtime." But "No books before nap" is a pretty stupid thing to say, and an even stupider thing to attempt to enforce. Even if I was exhausted, the five minutes it took to snuggle and read meant everything to her. Why I had attempted to deny that for even a moment is beyond me. There is no harm in reading a book while snuggling, and it is best to capitulate to positive requests than be stoic.

I told you this story, because it explains the benefits you receive in being a younger sibling. Basically, I get to make more mistakes with Sister, and then hopefully do better by you.

(And better by her, in the future.)

Hopefully, I made everything up to Sister after her nap. That's when I gleefully accepted a request to show her how to hula hoop.

"Daddy is silly!" she informed me as I floundered.

Yes, he is.

But mostly because he is uncoordinated. You'll learn that soon enough if you ask me to help you practice football, baseball, or any sport you might find yourself interested in.

Love,

Dad

February 20

Hey Buddy...

I am in South Bend, Indiana, and finally have a couple of days to sit, reflect, and write to you about what happened at the beginning of the month.

On Tuesday, February second, you woke up in the middle of the night with a dramatic cough. Very dramatic. So much so that Mommy ran you to the emergency room, where they gave you a steroid shot and an epinephrine breathing treatment. The doctors gave Mommy instructions on how to handle another cough attack, and felt that the trip to the ER wasn't unwise, per se, but neither was it overly necessary. Basically, a steamy bathroom could have cleared up your cough.

You went to daycare, acted normal, and all was well.

On Wednesday, February third, you woke up crying.

This is (sadly) normal for you, and Mommy was unconcerned as she entered your room. Unconcerned, that is, until she picked you up. You had a blistering fever, and you were panting.

Using the instructions we had been given, Mommy sat in the bathroom with you for 20 minutes, the shower on full-blast hot to create steam. When that didn't work I took you into the garage: first hot, then cold air to shock your little lungs.

Neither did anything to improve your breathing, so Mommy took you to urgent care. I was to gather up Sister and follow along after getting breakfast into her.

We got to urgent care about thirty minutes after you and Mommy, but that was well long enough. Your breathing was horrendous, your fever high, and your oxygen levels low. You were lethargic, and at one point went limp. They wanted to call an ambulance and take you back to the ER.

I was stunned, and mentally shut down a little. I wanted to believe the previous diagnosis was accurate and worth listening to; the ER doctors had poo-pooed everything, saying you were fine. They wouldn't have sent you home if it were serious, right? I couldn't wrap my mind around the fact you were in danger, and asked for a second opinion. We called your regular pediatrician. I figured we could go see him, he'd laugh off the opinion of the urgent care trainee, and all would be well in our world.

That didn't happen.

Instead, your regular nurse took the call and she doubled-down on the decision to call an ambulance, so Mommy had urgent care call 911 as I rushed Sister to daycare. I returned just in time to see you being wheeled out on a gurney. You were wrapped in blankets, and all I could see was your face. You looked so tiny, so helpless, on the adult-sized stretcher. My heart dropped into my stomach and I wanted to cry and throw up at the same time. Mommy was right beside you, and we locked eyes. I could tell it was taking all her strength to not cry herself.

Mommy got into the ambulance with you, and they fired up the sirens and took off to the hospital. I followed as best I could, but wasn't sure I could disobey any of the traffic laws without reprimand and soon fell behind. After a fuckup by Google Maps, one that took me to the complete opposite end of the hospital and not the ER as I had requested—fuck you very much, technology—I made it to your side twenty minutes after you landed.

The doctors immediately drew blood, ordered X-rays and an IV, and set about trying to figure out what was wrong with you. You were completely lethargic. Your head drooped, and you were listless and disinterested in the world around you. Your fever was 104 degrees, which was insanely high and frighteningly worrisome. To make matters worse—because of course things can always be worse—your heart was pumping like mad. At one point it reached 225 beats per minute, causing an alarm to sound and the word "TACHYCARDIA" to flash on the monitor.

Mommy held you tight and cooed to you; whispering into your ear to calm you. It worked, and your heart rate went from "freak out" high back to "crazy" high. By then, the decision had been made to admit you. The doctors had no clue what was going on—the X-rays were clean—but they didn't want such a sick baby to be away from monitoring and immediate professional care.

At this point, I made a quick trip home to pack an overnight bag for Mommy, and returned just as the two of you were being taken upstairs to the hospital proper.

The next few days are pretty much a blur.

Aunt Jessica came and spent one night at our house, then took Sister with her back to Des Moines for her first ever sleepover away from home. Sister had visited you in the hospital, but had no real clue what was happening. She knew that you were "sick," she just didn't know what that meant. Unfortunately, neither did the doctors, actually. Despite their best efforts, they couldn't determine exactly what you had. Even worse, on Thursday, you got worse.

You were given a feeding tube. You were given a breathing tube. You were given a tube to remove air from your stomach. You were attached to machines to monitor your oxygen saturation, heart rate, and every other statistic possible. In no time at all you were a mess of wires, tubes, gauze, and stickers holding the aforementioned tubes and wires to your face. It was heartbreaking, but worse, you barely seemed to notice or mind. You were just vacant. Your eyes were languid, your body a lump, and you couldn't sleep for more than thirty minutes a pop.

It was, in a word, fucking awful.

OK, that's two words, but you get the picture.

Your fever refused to break; it hovered around 104 degrees, and had been there for over twenty-four hours. That's dangerous for an adult, much less a one-and-a-half year old. You continued to breathe as if you'd just finished running a marathon, and your heart pounded near 190 beats per minute instead of the normal 100.

On Thursday night the decision was made to start you on antibiotics. The doctors still hadn't officially diagnosed you, but you weren't improving. Something had to be done. If it was a virus, the medicine wouldn't do anything, but it wouldn't harm you. If it was a bacterial infection—as your doctor suspected but couldn't confirm; the X-ray showed no pneumonia, but she felt strongly that it just wasn't showing up on film—you'd start to recover within hours.

Thankfully, she made the right decision.

On Friday, your fever eased ever-so-slightly to 102, and your breathing and heart rate inched toward normal. You showed an interest in nursing, so your feeding tube was removed to make way for Mommy's boob. You were doing so much better that you even slept a whopping three hours in a row. Yeah, I know that sounds like nothing, but after two days of thirty-minute naps, it was a godsend to everyone.

On Saturday, miraculously, it was all over. You turned a corner somewhere overnight; there's no other way to explain it. Your fever dropped, so on Saturday morning the final tubes came out and everyone waited breathlessly to see what would happen.

And what did happen?

You immediately wanted to get up and walk around. You still had your IV in, so Mommy or I alternately pushed the IV pole beside you as you walked, and you instinctively found your way to the play room and started busying yourself with the bounty of toys available. As you pushed a toy lawnmower down the hallway, your doctor saw you and stopped in her tracks.

"Is that Truman?!" she asked incredulously. "I think we should get that boy home!"

She was so relieved. In fact, everyone involved was so calm and professional, that it was only after the fact that we learned how worried everyone had been. You were sicker than they let on, because they knew having two completely panicked parents would be a disaster. More so than the two confused and worried parents we already were.

After several days of having fantastic medical care mere feet away, Mommy and I were a little afraid of leaving. We feared the isolation our home brought, as opposed to the security of having nurses and doctors on call 24/7. But, fears are to be overcome, so we packed up you and all your new toys—several of my friends, Travis, Mike, and Andy, had pitched in and bought you an enormous toy giraffe—and took you home.

The giraffe, by the way, brought many tourists to your room. Apparently it carried a hefty price tag and had been in the gift shop forever. When it was finally purchased, the entire hospital staff wanted to see where it ended up.

(Not for nothing, my nurse friend Tiny ordered several little plush toys for you. She lives in California, and has never even met you, but her heart was so moved by your plight that she wanted to reach out somehow. Suffice to say, I have great friends. As does Mommy; her friends brought us several meals while we were cooped up with you. We owe them a debt of gratitude we will never be able to repay.)

We never found out what you had, by the way. Best guess is that you had bacterial pneumonia, but it could've also been a virus that just happened to run its course at the same time you started antibiotics. Given that you got better immediately after, it was still the right decision by a mile.

One last item of note from this whole ordeal: When we arrived at the hospital, in the ER you sat on Mommy's lap the entire time. When you transferred upstairs, she both rode on the gurney with you and then went right into the crib with you. When Mommy needed a break or ran home for a nap and shower, I sat in there with you.

(When I say "crib," by the way, don't picture a traditional baby crib. It was a hospital bed, but a tiny, child-sized one. Mommy and I were cramped as could be, yes, but it was sturdy enough for us.)

Given that you had absolutely no clue what was happening to you — why strangers were constantly poking and prodding you, combined with the fact you were miserable — the least we felt we could do was be right there next to you the entire time. Not just spiritually, but physically. We wanted you to feel us, to know

96

that we were literally there with you. Not outside the bed holding your hand, but full-body there. In fact, the only time you actually slept, you did so leaning back against Mommy or me as if we were a recliner. Being in the crib with you wasn't anything Mommy and I discussed, it was just something we did. It seemed nothing short of appropriate to climb in next to you.

The staff found this strange. They said that on occasion a parent might sit in the crib for a little while, but never constantly like we did with you. They said they'd definitely never seen a parent sleep in the crib with their child. So… yeah. Remember that when you're sixteen and we're saying, "Goddammit, no. I already said you can't have the car tonight, so stop asking."

Heh.

Oh, I almost forgot: the day you got admitted to the hospital? That happened to be one day before we were scheduled to fly to California to visit Graw Diane.

I guess I owe you one, because you got us out of a family vacation.

A one-and-a-half year old and a three-and-a-half year old on an airplane?

Ugh. What torture that would have been.

Good looking out, Buddy.

Love,

Dad

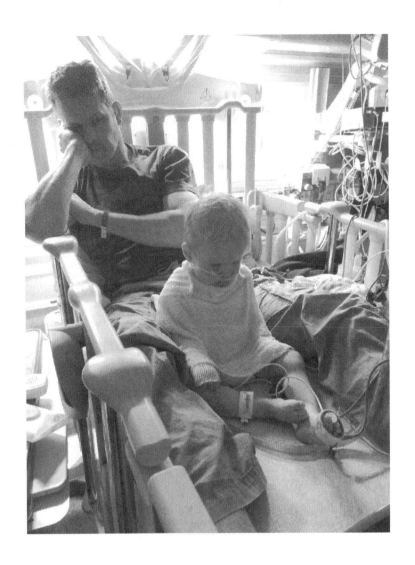

February 26

Hey Buddy...

I am in Fort Wayne, Indiana.

One thing I like about this club is that I feel I really earned my headlining slot here. A few years ago I was brought in as the middle, act. I had a great weekend, and after it was over the headliner said, "I never want to have to follow you again."

It was a great compliment, because it meant I made him work hard to win the audience over.

Unfortunately, the owner wasn't around that weekend, so he didn't see me. This meant that even though the booking agent was ready to move me up, the owner wasn't.

Fair enough.

I went back again in the same position and like before, at the end of the week the headliner asked, "Why aren't you closing this room?" Unlike before, this time the owner was around, and I was moved up for my next appearance. And, like I said, it feels nice to know you really earned something.

Which brings us to tonight.

While I was on stage, I saw the owner of the club enter the showroom. This is normal; sometimes managers/owners like to get a read on the comedian and watch the audience react while the comedian is on stage. Generally the owner will make a pass through the room, maybe watch what's happening for a minute or two, and then head back to the office to handle the business of paying bills. This owner, however, sat down. He sat down at the comic's table next to the emcee, and watched me.

Now, even though I'm comfortable on stage in front of audiences of any size, I have to admit that like anyone, I am susceptible to a touch of worker's anxiety; everyone wants to impress the boss. Instead of just telling my jokes, now I was telling my jokes while keeping one eye on the owner.

He stayed at the table for about 20 minutes. Every time I glanced his way, his eyes were on me. He was focused on what I was doing, listening to the laughter I was generating.

(Fortunately, I was having a great night. There was much in the way of laughter, and many applause breaks.)

I eventually left the stage, sold my wares to those who were buying, and when all was said and done talked to the host of the show. Without prompting, he told me: "I've worked here ten years and never seen the owner do that. Never seen him just sit down and watch a comic." When I asked why he thought the owner did it tonight, he said, "Because you're different. You're different from ninety percent of what comes through here. So many comics... you can just figure out their jokes or punchlines. Not yours. You surprise him."

As I said atop this note: pretty cool. Pretty cool indeed.

Love,

Dad

March 19

Hey Buddy...

I am in Pawnee City, Nebraska. I performed at a vineyard earlier, which I have to say is an oddity for the Midwest. When you think wine, you think California, or France, not Nebraska.

It was a fun show, but that's not what's on my mind. Right now, I'm thinking of a show from a couple of years ago, a time before you were even born.

Many negative words have been written about Millennials, which is a group of people born a few generations before you, also known as the "Participation Ribbon" generation. For the most part, I have tried not to be a grumpy old man in this situation.

I read about the student who sued his professor over a bad grade, and shrugged it off as an isolated incident.

I heard first-hand from a manager who received a phone call from an employee's mother, because he gave the Gen-Y employee a less-than-stellar performance review, and laughed at it.

I even rolled my eyes at the tale of a mother accompanying her son to a job interview, and the kid wondering why he didn't get said job.

But when I heard comedian Chris Rock say, "I won't work colleges anymore, because they've gotten too conservative," I paused.

In his own words: "Not in their political views — not like they're voting Republican — but in their social views and their willingness not to offend anybody. Kids raised on a culture of 'We're not going to keep score in the game because we don't want anybody to lose.' Or just ignoring race to a fault. You can't say 'the black kid over there.' No, it's 'the guy with the red shoes.' You can't even be offensive on your way to being inoffensive."

This frightened me, because if an icon like Chris Rock had to be worried about offending kids, what hope is there for a comedian of my limited stature?

As it turns out, none.

A couple of years ago I performed at a local university, and it was an unmitigated disaster.

Or so I was told.

I thought I was receiving a typical college response; the instant the lights went down, I heard nothing but students talking over me. When I said my first "Hello!" into the microphone, approximately 3 of 150 people in attendance responded. The rest were in their own world, eating, talking, and posting selfies to Instagram.

I shrugged it off and barreled forward the best I could, because I was under contract. I had to sling my jokes for thirty minutes, audience indifference be damned. It was with genuine surprise when, twenty-five minutes later, I was pulled from the stage. The student organization president told me I was "offending people."

I'm not dense. I knew I wasn't killing it. Had the apathy started halfway through my set, I would have said, "Oh crap, I'm losing them!" Since disinterest was the norm from the get go, I figured, "This is how it's going to be." But never in a million years did I think I was upsetting the audience.

When I was told otherwise, I asked which of my comments were out of line. Her opening response was: "Off the top of my head? When you made fun of white people names."

To be fair, I did make fun of white people names.

After the audience ignored my "Hello," it was obvious they weren't going to pay attention to me telling jokes. Given that, I decided to speak with them, to do interactive material. I started working the room, dancing on verbal eggshells the whole time. I am not stupid; I knew going in I would have to tread lightly.

For fifteen minutes I spoke with different tables, different students, making light, situational jokes: "You only ate half a baby carrot? You were too full to finish a baby carrot?"

(Groundbreaking? No. Safe? Yes. Hilarious? No. Chuckles from the six kids paying attention? Yes.)

When I got to a table of white girls, I figured I could be slightly more daring. And by slightly, I mean 0.5 on a scale of one to ten.

"What's your name?" I asked the first girl.

"Rachel," she responded.

"Oh God..." I groaned, over-emphasizing my exasperation to show I was being absurd. "That is the whitest name, ever."

I heard mild giggles from the peanut gallery, and the girls at the table laughed, so all was well.

Or, as stated, so I thought.

When that moment came back to bite me in the butt, I was floored. I asked for clarification—how it was offensive?—and was told, "The event is multicultural. Our goal is one hundred percent inclusivity." Pointing out any race, even my own, brought attention to race, which automatically "made things uncomfortable."

Though I didn't, I wanted to shout, "FOR WHO?!" I've been a comedian long enough to know the difference between comfortable and uncomfortable laughter, and the chuckle I heard at my comment was genuine.

The other "point of offense" is one I should have seen coming. Up front I wondered whether or not I should do a joke in support of gay marriage.

Now, as you read this, marriage equality will have been the norm for many years. But as I write it, the whole concept is actually new. That's right, for many years the American government dictated that marriage was a union between a man and a woman.

Think that's odd? Before 1967, interracial marriage was illegal. Yup, America has always been on the wrong side of progress, and our government has legislated in favor of racism and homophobia repeatedly over the course of history. Even worse, these subjects aren't going away anytime soon, because people exist who believe that love should be dictated and controlled.

During this point in time, marriage equality for the LGBTQ community was a hot topic, and I was performing jokes in favor of it. My jokes attacked bigotry and backwards ways of thinking.

But that said, I still wasn't sure whether or not I should tell such jokes in a college atmosphere. Why? Because people hear trigger words and react to them, not the context in which they are being used. They don't listen to the whole of a sentence or idea; they tune out the instant they hear one thing they don't like.

Scary, but true.

Instead of yanking the joke, I instead went crystal clear, adding a preface up front. Speaking slowly and clearly, I started the joke with: "I'll tell you this; I support marriage equality, and I don't understand the arguments against marriage equality..."

(Note: I didn't say "gay marriage," I made sure to say "marriage equality." I was being very politically correct for the sensitive little snowflakes in front of me.)

While being lectured after the show, I was told: "The problem is with you, a heterosexual male talking about gay marriage in the first place. You cannot determine how someone who is homosexual will react to your stance on their issue."

Hearing that, I was at a loss for words.

If my joke had been at the expense of homosexuality, then yes, it would have been out of line. Not just at the university, but in general; making fun of a persecuted group of people is in extremely poor taste. But to say I cannot talk about the subject? That's bullshit. Especially because the LGBTQ community needs me to talk about it. Not as a comedian, but as a straight person. The only way bigotry will end in America is by having straight people standing side-by-side with the LGBTQ community, championing their causes. The majority has to see and understand the plight of the minority in order to create change. If the LGBTQ community were to stand alone, any issues would be dismissed as "a gay problem."

(Just like AIDS was "a gay problem" in the 1980s, before whoops!, straights started dying from it, too. I'm sure you'll learn a glossed over version of that lovely slice of American history in school.)

Anyway, logical failings aside, if there was a viewpoint I thought would be safe on a college campus, it would be pro-marriage equality. But no. Even the topic is verboten, meaning the line was crossed when I opened my mouth. What came out of it didn't matter.

What's "funny," and by that I mean "not funny at all," is that when I was removed from the stage, I had been doing material involving you and Sister for about ten minutes. It's probably the safest material I have, with nothing remotely controversial contained within. In fact, not only is it not controversial, it's deeply personal material, and at times empathetic. How often do you see a comedian tell an audience he and his wife are donating embryos to an infertile couple? I'm guessing never. I do, and it generally gets a nice pop of laughter at the end, too. I mean, not at this show, with all the texting and ignoring... but when an audience is engaged, yeah, they laugh.

Unfortunately, no one had the wits about them to realize, "OK, he's transitioned. No more hot topics like 'gay marriage' or 'white people names.'" Likewise, no one had the decency or common sense to think, "You know what, he only has five minutes left, let him finish." Because when you're not paying attention to content and you're simply trying to indulge the delicate sensibilities of a society waiting to be outraged, you've already lost.

I will admit: in some teeny-tiny way, I understand where the "fear of offending" comes from at a university. Many are taxpayer-funded institutions, and when someone gets upset it might end up in the newspaper. Then donors get angry, and the governor gets involved, and blahblahblah...

I get that.

But you cannot cater to everyone, and everyone is offended by something. That's simply life.

My hope is that my experience was an isolated incident.

My fear is that this is the future, with over-the-top sensitivity a new normal that uses good intentions as a weapon to destroy society. After all, we know good intentions are exactly what the road to hell is paved with.

I do not know what society will be like when you are aware enough to read this, but I am pretty sure racism, sexism, and homophobia will still exist. They've been around since the dawn of time, and they'll be around until the sun burns out.

It is your duty to speak out against them; you cannot sit idle by and let inequality go unchallenged. Maybe you will run into indifference and interference, like I did at this show, but you cannot let that deter you.

Also, and this is important: don't be reactionary. Always listen for context and content. Don't jump to conclusions, and don't be someone who is "triggered" by a word or subject you might not like. Take the time to digest the whole of a situation, and draw conclusions based on reflection, not knee-jerk reaction.

Up top, I said that I try not to be a grumpy old man when dealing with younger generations. One thing I keep in mind when dealing with people like the student-body president who chastised me is this: she didn't raise herself. No child ever becomes who they are on their own. Someone raised Millennials and instilled quirks and sensitivities in them. It's easy to make fun of them for getting participation ribbons and attaboys for doing nothing, but who hands those ribbons out? What parent first decided their precious child couldn't endure hurt feelings, and why did the rest of society go along with that?

I don't know, but I'm going to try and do better by you.

Love,

Dad

March 26

Hey Buddy...

I am in Minneapolis, thinking of my past.

When I started writing letters to you, I knew that at some point I would have to cover a few harsh topics. Tonight, I am tackling a very difficult issue.

I grew up not knowing what domestic abuse was.

I didn't witness it in my home, and didn't hear much about it in my social circles or the media. Back then, it was "something people didn't talk about."

Thankfully, social norms are changing. You will be fully aware of domestic violence, and furthermore (and more importantly) your role in preventing it. I want you to be ready to act if ever presented with a horrible situation, if only because I wasn't.

I have been witness to two instances of domestic violence in my life. It is easily two too many, and at each occurrence I probably failed in my duty to do the right thing.

The first happened when I was in college.

I lived in Milwaukee, Wisconsin; my roommates were Jack— someone from my hometown—and Matt, a stranger.

Matt arrived via a vacancy in the apartment and a subsequent ad placed on the student housing board. Matt's girlfriend, Susan, had seen the ad, contacted me, and basically done all the legwork for Matt. She was, sad to say, his doormat.

Matt was affable enough, but in a dimwitted way. By that, I mean he didn't have his shit together. Matt got drunk nightly, his credit rating was in the toilet, and his car was about to be repossessed. He was both a waiter, and enrolled in the police academy; Matt wanted to be a cop.

To say Matt and Susan had an unhealthy relationship would be an understatement. He cheated on her constantly, and a multitude of women called the apartment nightly. Back then cell phones didn't exist, so they left message after message on our answering machine—an external, old-school version of "voicemail." Since anyone could play/hear answering machine messages—the answering machine was in a public room in our apartment—Matt would try to delete any from his many side "girlfriends" before Susan came over.

When off cheating on Susan, he would stay out late, leaving her to call repeatedly into the wee hours, sobbing: "Matt... it's three a.m., where are you?"

Matt would return home drunk, laughing as he listened to her growing ever-more-anxious voice.

When they fought, I rolled my eyes. I thought they were perfectly damaged and wonderfully stupid enough for one another. She pined for him, and he treated her like garbage. You could set your watch by their arguments, whether on the phone or in person. They were in the middle of a particularly heated argument in Matt's bedroom when it happened. Both were yelling, and Susan was crying.

I remember it clearly; the sound of a slab of meat being slapped down on a butcher's counter pierced the shouting.

The fighting stopped.

Everything went dead silent.

I froze.

He just hit her.

The certainty of that thought sat in my mind for about ten seconds, then I stood up calmly and walked to Jack's room. I knocked on his door and he opened it, innocently asking, "What's up?"

"Matt just hit Susan," I explained. "Do you want to deal with him, or take her home?"

Jack didn't flinch. "I'll get her out of here."

There was no discussion between us, no wondering what to do or hemming and hawing. We went to Matt's room and gave them no choice in the matter: Susan was being escorted out, and he was staying behind with me.

I sat Matt down, and if he said anything I don't remember what it was. Did he apologize, or feel guilty? The gray matter in my head hasn't retained that knowledge. I told Matt he was done, that he had to be out by the end of the month. The sooner the better, in fact. Whatever happened wasn't going to take place under my roof again. I offered no second chance and waited for no penance.

Matt was gone shortly thereafter. I never heard from him or Susan again.

I did, unfortunately, learn something new while meandering down memory lane.

Wanting to get this story right, I emailed Jack and asked, "Hey, completely random, but do you remember if Susan said anything the night you gave her a ride home after Matt hit her?"

Jack responded, "Wow, that is random..." and then told me about a night he gave Susan a ride home after Matt had hit her.

Except it wasn't the night I was asking about.

Jack described a night memorable to him involving Matt's swinging fist, one I hadn't known about. This means the ugly episode happened more than once.

How sad.

The second instance of violence I was witness to...

...the backstory is almost too long and convoluted to explain.

I was in love with, and sleeping with, a woman named Judy. Judy was in love and in a cohabitating relationship with a lout named Jim.

Judy and I worked at a restaurant together.

One weekend she called in sick to every one of her shifts. Because of our "situation," she asked me to come visit her at home.

As it turned out, she wasn't sick. She was hiding.

When I arrived I knocked on the door with the innocence of ignorance and was greeted by horror. One of Judy's eyes was a swollen, purple mess. I was stunned. She had given me no heads up.

Judy actually half-laughed at my surprise, because she had gotten so used to seeing herself in that condition. To her credit, Judy didn't try to lie and say she fell down or any such nonsense. She owned right up and admitted Jim punched her. Judy did, sadly, brush aside my concerns with some of the ugliest words I've heard regarding domestic violence: "Oh, Jim never does this. I deserved it. I was egging him on..."

I deserved it. The statement made me want to throw up.

At the time, I felt powerless. I wanted to kill Jim, to be a champion and protector of the woman I treasured. Judy warned me not to do anything, because she loved Jim. She said she would never speak to me again if I went after him, and considering I was wrapped around her finger...

It's a pathetic, albeit honest, excuse for my inaction. In the end, I did the only thing I could, which was to remain her puppet. That's what made her happy, so that's the role I retained.

I'm not sure there is anything you can do for someone determined to stay in an abusive relationship. Should I have called the police on Matt, or Jim? I don't know. Considering neither Susan nor Judy would have pressed charges, it would have done nothing productive. I did the best I could at the time, even if it probably wasn't good enough.

I do, however, know this: violence begins at home, and I have you.

Maybe I didn't act as appropriately as I could have back then, but I can raise you to be better than the Matts and Jims of the world. Truman, you will be raised to respect women, to respect people. You will understand violence is an action of the weak, not a show of strength.

I can also make sure your sister knows that no matter what, no matter the heat of the moment or the passion involved, no hand should ever be raised against her. Furthermore, no matter what threats are made, she cannot be afraid to talk about violence or seek help, should something awful happen.

All lessons come from emulation. When you see me treating your mother with respect and love, you will expect and offer similar treatment in your own relationships. You will watch conflict-resolution between your parents take place verbally, not physically. There may be raised voices from time to time, but never a raised hand. Non-violence will be infused in your bones.

I will teach you the warning signs of an unhealthy relationship, so you may exit it before becoming mired in the disaster that was Matt and Susan, or Judy and Jim.

Which isn't to say domestic violence is easy. You can't just escape a harmful relationship; some people are possessive, and dangerous. But with increased public awareness of what domestic violence is, the less I hope it happens.

Domestic violence used to be something you didn't talk about. It was a "family issue." Whatever took place behind closed doors stayed behind closed doors.

No longer.

My hope is that as you age, more and more people will add their voices, and domestic violence will be something you read about in the history books, not the news. My fear is that we are moving too slowly in the right direction.

When I originally wrote up these tales, I submitted the essay to an online publication I have a weekly column with. Their response was: too controversial. While their mission statement literally reads, "We shy away from nothing," when presented with a story of domestic abuse, they cowered in fear. It was back to the old way of dealing with domestic abuse: subjects like this are best not talked about.

Fortunately, I was able to submit it to another, braver, publication, and they posted without hesitation. Their belief, like mine, is that the only way to change a behavior is to expose it. You have to share your stories so people don't feel so alone in the world.

The stories I have just told are my failure to do the right thing, and my contribution to the conversation. Even if they don't make a huge difference to others, they made a difference to me, and my experiences will help me raise you correctly.

Love,

Dad

April 2

Hey Buddy…

I just got back from Atlantic, Iowa, and have to admit that it was one hell of an interesting show.

The contract said the performance was at an Elk's Lodge or something similar. Moose Lodge? I've already forgotten.

When the other comedian and I arrived, we were immediately nervous. The average age of the audience was above seventy; the youngest person was still a grandparent by a mile. When we got the gig, no one informed us we would be telling jokes at a glorified retirement home.

To our mutual amazement, the show went great. The opening comic went up and did well, and then I went up and did exceedingly well. We were both stunned, which brings me to two clichéd sayings.

First, never judge a book by its cover. It's simplistic, yes, but sometimes simple messages carry the most meaning. You never know what's inside a book, just as you never know what's inside a person. Snap judgment upon anything only offers you the opportunity to miss out on greatness. We figured older folks wouldn't be up for our unique brands of humor, and we were wrong. Dead wrong.

Second, there is an old saying that respect is something to be earned, not given. I disagree, and that's absolutely not how I live my life. I think you greet everyone with equal respect, and it's theirs to lose.

If they do lose it — maybe they espouse racist or other sorts of awful beliefs — that's fine. You don't have to respect everyone; many people don't deserve it. But it should be offered up front.

I believe that by thinking others have to earn your respect, you demean them. You place yourself above, and that isn't how you enter into any relationship, be it a business partnership, a friendship, or even a casual interaction. By demanding people earn your respect, you immediately put them on the defensive, which will have negative consequences in the long run.

It's best to enter on equal terms, and try to maintain that balance as best you can.

I made a snap judgment of my audience tonight — I judged them by their appearance — which could have led to a horrible show. But by greeting them as equals — I'm here to entertain, and you're here to laugh, so let's have at it — everything worked out amazingly well.

So, yeah. Even in my mildly advanced years, I'm still figuring this shit out.

Love,

Dad

April 9

> *"My girlfriend is a vegetarian, which pretty much makes me a vegetarian."*
>
> ~ Jules Winnfield

Hey Buddy…

I am in St. Cloud, Minnesota.

When I moved to Iowa to be with your mom, I discovered she didn't know anything about the National Football League. Iowa has no professional-level teams, so college dominates everyone's corn-fed sporting consciousness.

On the first NFL Sunday of our cohabitation, I mentioned I was looking forward to watching football. Mommy was fine with that, so when noon rolled around I fired up the idiot box. Mommy puttered around the condo waiting for it to end, and as the game finished she said with a smile, "Great! Now let's go do something!"

I responded with a hesitant and somewhat confused point to the television, and grunted, "More. Football."

Mommy rolled her eyes and went back to killing time.

When the late game finished, she — slightly frustrated but still in kind spirits — said, "OK, most of the day is gone, but it's still salvageable…"

She had no clue there was a night game.

Without going into too much detail, yes, the exasperation played out again the next day: "Monday Night Football? When does it end?!"

(Again: Iowa. No professional sports.)

After that initial dive into the deep end of football, a bit of balancing took place. I no longer watch every single game possible, and Mommy has actually come to root for the Green Bay Packers, as I hope you and Sister do by the time you read this.

In short, your mom and I influenced one another.

That's what I believe relationships are about: influence, and enhancement. You change for and with your partner, while retaining all the qualities that make you, you. Those intangibles that make you attractive as a person are the reason your mate was interested in you in the first place.

It's a tricky balancing act, and not everyone is able to pull it off.

A friend of mine somehow retains her foundation, yet is a chameleon regarding every superficial interest possible. As she flitters between lovers, her activities shift to suit whomever she's with.

"My boyfriend likes hockey, so I love hockey! My new boyfriend hates hockey, so I hate hockey!"

And so on.

Yet, beneath all the external changes, she remains... her. Most of her interests mold into that of her lover, but not her personality.

I think that's fair game. Of course, some people go too far, get lost in relationships, and lose their identity in the process. Which is sad. When you give up your belief system, the people once closest to you notice.

I have a friend I don't interact much with anymore, someone who got into a relationship with a politically insane person. Where she once spoke rationally, now she spews crazy. My friend internalized her partner's madness, and I no longer recognize the person I knew/liked/respected for years. Sad, but I think it is a side effect of desperation. My friend had been through several failed relationships, and despair is a powerful force: "I better be super supportive of this one, and if I don't believe everything my lover does I'll be alone again..."

In a relationship, the weaker of the two personalities will always succumb to the stronger.

On the flip side of that example, I have a friend who is a 31-year-old virgin. He adamantly opposes changing anything about himself to suit a woman, and states so forcefully: "I will find someone who accepts me as is, and that's all there is to it."

Unfortunately, he's more Steve Buscemi than Brad Pitt. Only without Steve Buscemi's unique charm and likeability. Because he refuses to put in even the most minimal of effort to be interesting to anyone, he remains single. Even better, he sometimes gets angry about being single, blaming the women who don't see him for the magnificent creature he spies when looking in the mirror.

(Mommy issues, he's got 'em.)

Again, it's about balance. You have to transform, while still retaining your integrity. You can make major changes and keep hold of your inner essence, but only if those changes are positive; change is supposed to be progressive, not regressive.

I'm a walking model of enormous affirmative change. This might be odd for you to read, but my whole life, I never had an interest in babies or kids. I was beyond vocal with my opinion. Then, when we were still dating, Mommy put her foot down: if she was to become my wife, we were going to become parents.

I relented, and though it could be labeled as hypocrisy — me flipping on everything I had once stood for — becoming a father didn't alter my personality in any way but positively.

In fact, having you and Sister has been the most helpful, life-affirming change I have ever undertaken. Ninety-nine percent of my friends recognize and revel in this. Some mock me playfully; others simply take joy in the new-yet-old me. One has even said I flipped him to the dark side. Once as adamantly against children as I was, watching me experience joy — combined with him finding a woman he truly loves — he now shouts, "I can't wait to be a father!"

Change is about meeting in the middle, with occasional trips to the far side of the other when it's important. The trick is knowing what is sacrifice, and what is generosity. Becoming a father might look like sacrifice to some on the outside, but to me it was a generous giving of self. Sometimes when you become more like your partner, you lose things you never really needed in the first place.

The long and short of all this is: everything in life is about balance. Do not become a shadow of your former self when you enter a relationship, and do not dominate your partner.

Grow together.

Influence one another, and be happy.

Love,

Dad

April 20

Hey Buddy…

I am in Dubuque, Iowa, smiling while I write.

It has begun, the process of you emulating your sister. I didn't know when it would happen, but it is an adorable little phase you are in.

Since she could speak, Sister would see an airplane in the sky and yell "Airplane!" Now, you follow suit, doing the best you can, shouting "Airpane!"

(That's right, "airpane." You're not sure about your "Ls" yet, which to a parent makes your point-and-shout all the more adorable.)

The two of you also scan the daytime sky for the moon, and when you find it you draw out the "Os," saying "Moooooooon!" excitedly.

The two of you doing these things bursts my heart, growing it 3x every time.

Another way you emulate is upon departure from our house. When we leave, we generally give our mini-schnauzer, Kitty, a treat. It's a way of assuaging the pain he feels when he's abandoned at home, and good for a momentary distraction while we scoot out the door.

Sister, for a while — and for no reason — would put the treat on her head, and then jump and let it fall off onto the floor. It made no sense, but she did it anyway. I would hand her the treat, she would place it upon her head, hop, and then giggle as it tumbled off her head and Kitty gobbled it up.

I would roll my eyes and say, "You know, you can just hand it to him..."

Sister would shake her head and smile. Whatever she was doing made sense to her, and her alone.

Now you have begun putting the treat on your head, for absolutely no reason, and jumping so it falls off and to the floor. I shake my head in amused confusion, because it utterly bewilders me as to why this is the preferred method of treat-delivery, but such is life.

These days, your sister is into learning Kitty's abilities — the tricks Mommy taught him long ago. She holds the treat in her hand, pointing at Kitty with the other and shouting "Sit! Sit!"

So Kitty sits, and she keeps yelling "Sit! Sit!" which leaves our poor dog confused. You can see it in his earthen eyes, filled with longing for the biscuit as he thinks: "I'm already sitting... I can't sit any further."

Eventually your sister drops the treat, and Kitty is paid for his patience.

Naturally, you have begun holding the treat and yelling "Sit" as best you can, followed by putting the treat on your head (for absolutely no reason) and then jumping so it slides off you and onto the floor. You don't even actually wait for Kitty to sit; you just shout it because it's something your sister does.

It is wonderfully adorable.

I have no idea how long this emulation phase lasts, how long you two will be peas and carrots. At some point, I am unfortunately certain you will part ways, fight over toys, fight over the remote, fight over whatever it's possible for siblings to fight over...

...and my heart will break.

So I will enjoy this while I can.

Love,

Dad

April 29

Hey Buddy...

I'm in Minneapolis, but yesterday you and I were playing in the basement at home.

You were doing your Truman thing as *Zenyatta Mondatta* played in the background, and for a majority of the song "Voices Inside My Head" you acted like the music wasn't even playing. But holy poop-on-a-stick, when Sting started yelling "Sha!" you broke into a wide smile and started shouting right along with him.

"Sha! Sha! Sha!"

I couldn't help but laugh. I don't know how many times you had heard the song—maybe once or twice at best, but while most words escape you, sounds like that you can mimic quite well.

Because I am trying to shield you from all things awful, you don't listen to "kid" music; instead, you have an appreciation for The Police. Whenever "Roxanne" comes on, your face lights up and your eyes look around for the speaker, as if you actually want to see the music exiting it.

You begin a little bounce-dance, where your feet are rooted to the floor, but you bop at the knees, smiling and bouncing along to Sting's lament for his red-light lover.

You've actually begun singing the last word of many songs Sister likes. Because she asks me to play them repeatedly, you hear them repeatedly, and thus learn them. So when we're in the car and "Hello!" (from The Book of Mormon soundtrack) comes on, you spend the entire song singing individual words from the end of each line. It's hilarious.

The song will start, and the speakers emanate: "Hello, my name is Elder Price, and I would like to share with you the most amazing book..."

A second after that last word, "BOOK!" will sound from the back seat, from your little vocal cords.

(My favorite part, of course, is hearing you shout "Jesus!" after, "Would you like a free book written by Jesus?")

As of late, Sister has been particularly obsessed with "Monkey Wrench," by the Foo Fighters.

Gonna be interesting seeing if you can keep up with that song.

Love,

Dad

May 6

Hey Buddy…

I am in Milwaukee, Wisconsin. I spent a good chunk of my life here — some time in elementary school, and then again for college. Most of the 1990s, in fact. While there are many tales of my life from that time, most of them have already been written — examined to death as I continually try to figure out who I am as a person and post and publish my thoughts as blogs and books.

So what am I writing about today? Well, it's a cheat. Sunday is Mother's Day, a Hallmark holiday invented to sell flowers and cards and to give the brunch business a boost at local restaurants.

(I'm not knocking Mother's Day, exactly, it's just that being a mom is a full-time job. Celebrating it one day a year is a bit silly. Moms deserve to be championed daily, but that's another story.)

Last year… or maybe the year before, a blogger group in Iowa City held a contest: write about a "Super Mom," and win gifts if crowned champion.

I entered the contest, and wrote the following about your mom:

Lydia Fine is a Super Mom because she convinced me to become a dad.

My whole life, I didn't want kids. I saw them as money and time drains. This was all rooted in personal issues and a childhood not worth going into, but when Lydia and I started dating we seemed to be on the same page.

131

"Do you want kids?"

"Nope. You?"

"Nope."

Boom, win.

Unfortunately, that wonderful power known as "The Biological Clock" soon started ticking, and Lydia realized the only reason she had never wanted kids was because she hadn't been in a loving relationship yet. Once she discovered the joy of a union devoid of drama and nonsense, she knew the only thing that could make a coupling better was a family.

So, before we were married, she told me: "This is a deal breaker. No babies, no me."

I was intimidated, but ensnared. I put all my previous fears on hold because I understood that if I let her slip through my fingers I would never find love again.

Sadly, it turned out making babies wasn't as easy for us as for your average high school student. Lydia couldn't ovulate; she could make the eggs, but they wouldn't travel down the fallopian tube to be fertilized. Infertility was a struggle for several years of our marriage, and through it all Lydia was stalwart. Through the struggles, she had her eye on the prize, and never gave up.

Our daughter, Hillary, was born two-and-a-half years ago. Our son Truman followed two years later.

There is a philosophy that argues that when you earn something, rather than having it given to you, you respect your accomplishment more.

Lydia respects her position as a mother. She fought for it every step of the way, and shines bright in the role.

I travel for work, and Lydia takes on "single" mom duties full-force every weekend I am away. Feeding, bathing, clothing... Given that our daughter is two-and-a-half, it's like dealing with a mini-diva. Irrational demands, specific hairstyle instructions — "NO MOMMY! TWO PONYTAILS, NOT THREE!" — a mood that changes on a whim... The only difference between our daughter and Jennifer Lopez is that our daughter wears Elmo panties, and is a decent singer.

On top of that, our son refuses to sleep for more than two hours a stretch. Lydia gets up with him every single time. Breastfeeding is that important to her. When he refused to take solids — and by "refused" I mean he swung his left hook at any spoon anywhere near his face — Lydia kept at it. Where I had given up long ago, Lydia persisted, and after weeks of failed attempts finally got Truman to chow down on solid food.

Little Truman endured seven straight weeks of ear infections before he was able to get tubes. Once again, Daddy was off wandering for work, so Lydia attended the minor surgery alone with him. Ever the strong woman, Lydia is constantly taking on all the duties she has to so her kids get whatever it is they need.

Lydia deals with all of the above with the grace of a ballet dancer and patience of a saint.

And, all of the above aside, as stated: she gave me the opportunity to be a father.

I owe her everything for that.

If she hadn't pushed, I might have never known what it is to be a dad, and I would be an incomplete person because of that.

They say that behind every good man is a great woman. I say nonsense. My wife isn't operating from the shadows; she is front and center, leading by example. Imagine what good she will instill into our children, given she will place her values into them from birth, considering the way she was able to shape me, a grown adult.

Just imagine.

*   *   *

For the record, this essay won.

Mom got a free massage, and several other gifts.

Oh, and she got the title of "Super Mom" for a full year.

Because she is a Super Mom.

Don't ever forget that.

Love,

Dad

May 13

Hey Buddy...

I was farting around online and saw a video going viral. A woman at a chain of stores called Walmart berated a man for using government subsidized food assistance to buy his items, and another customer filmed the interaction and posted it online.

To be honest, I prefer it when bunnies or puppies go viral, but I guess sometimes it has to be bitter and rude people.

While watching the video, three thoughts popped into my noggin:

- Of course he's paying with food stamps. He's at Walmart. (Snarky and mean, yes, but the stand-up comic in me always comes out first, and truth be told, Walmart owns 18% of the food stamp market. While Coke and Pepsi fight for fractions of a business percentage, Walmart has the food stamp crowd in the palm of their corporate hand.)

- Lady, you're shopping at Walmart. How is your unique brand of white trash any better than anyone else's? (Again, snotty, but come on. There's a reason there's a website called "People of Walmart" and not "People of Target.")

- I have seen people pay for their purchases using food assistance before, and it never once crossed my mind to belittle them. In fact, the only thought I've ever had is: There but for the grace of God go I.

The last thought lingers, because it isn't a throwaway like the first two.

I do not understand how people develop. I don't know if it is nature, or nurture, that cultivates or lets wither emotions such as sympathy, empathy, or compassion. I don't know what causes one person to see someone in need and become outraged while another feels fortunate.

What I try to remember is: I don't know anyone's story. I don't know if a person on food stamps was laid off or could only find a job that didn't cover all the bills. I don't know if someone homeless was abused as a child and ran away to escape violence. I don't know if they used alcohol or drugs to ease their pain. I do not know what put anyone on the path to need, and I don't really care.

I see a fellow human, and that is enough.

It is, I believe, rare to start with everything and throw it all away and end up on assistance. It is very easy, however, to begin life in a less-than-ideal situation and get trapped in the cycle of poverty.

The video is truncated, meaning I cannot tell who started what. Reports say the woman told her son—loudly enough to be heard—"This is why you go to college, so you don't take handouts."

This leads me to believe that compassion is a taught, or learned, behavior. I think, or maybe I hope, that we are born inherently good; that a child will see someone hurting and feel sadness because of the situation, not anger at the other person for their need.

If that's the case, the woman yelling at the man on assistance is failing her son. She is teaching him condescension, not compassion, meaning the cycle of judgment and ridicule will probably be passed on to the next generation.

What I found odd was the fact the woman didn't seem to understand that she is more of a problem than the man on assistance. As she is shopping at Walmart, she is actively supporting what she's railing against.

Walmart is known for opening locations at an enormous cost to taxpayers. Cities provide utility work and tax breaks, and then because of the low wages it pays employees, they need food stamps to get by. The group Americans for Tax Fairness estimates Walmart costs taxpayers $6.2 billion a year when broken down into categories such as food stamps, Medicaid, and subsidized housing. So shopping there promotes corporate welfare, and that costs taxpayers much more than citizens on assistance do. But all this is somewhat beside the point, if indeed I do have one.

I guess I just don't understand what makes one person compassionate and understanding and another bitter and useless. An ivory tower of self-righteousness gave the woman all the ammunition she needed to berate someone trying to feed his family, even though she knew nothing about him.

Does the man work 50 hours a week like he says in the video? Maybe. Is he an addict who spends his money on drugs? Maybe.

I don't know, and I don't care.

You know what I saw when I watched the video? That man's son sitting in the grocery cart.

Not only did the woman expose her own poor parenting skills by being horrible in public, she tried to shame that man in front of his son.

A child. A child who didn't deserve any of what she offered. A child whose father was doing what he could to feed him, even if that meant going on government assistance.

Children are influenced the most by what they experience at home. Right now, it's depressing to think there are people out there like that woman, someone raising a son who will grow up believing it's OK to treat people like they're disposable. Maybe that's how her parents raised her, in a manner opposite "judge not lest ye." If so, that's unfortunate, but damaged cycles are meant to be broken, not passed down as heirlooms.

Truman, it is my job to teach you (and Sister) compassion and non-judgment. You never know a person's story, so it is best to look upon them with empathetic, not angry, eyes. Think again to the phrase above: There but for the grace of God go I. That message will be one of the most important beliefs I instill in you.

You are important, special, and I love you. It might be the case that not everyone received the same kind of attention during their childhood. Always keep that in mind when you see someone in dire straits.

Love,

Dad

May 21

Hey Buddy…

I am in Indianapolis, Indiana, thinking about something that happened earlier in the week.

Every so often, I'm afforded the opportunity to take a side gig that doesn't involve comedy. A part time or temp job — something that adds to the bank account, but doesn't infringe upon my ability to up and away to another town to tell jokes. For a while I was a substitute teacher, and I've worked in offices. This month, I was able to make a few extra bucks working for a special census. A town close to ours wanted a head count, and I was able to latch on to a position with the government for a few weeks.

When people I'm working with find out I'm a comedian, they're generally curious. We usually strike up a fairly decent conversation on the topic. Rarely, but every so often, something goes awry. This week was one of those times.

A coworker asked if my act was "clean." Because that means something different to everyone, I asked for her definition of "clean." Her response was: "Do you use the F-word?"

I explained that while it's not a staple of my act, every so often it makes for a decent insert. Sometimes you test words, and a nice F-bomb adds a bit of spice in a sentence. A little flavor, if you will. In my opinion, swearing can provide emphasis where necessary, but shouldn't be a crutch to fall back on or a comma to be overused.

The woman explained that if she hears the word, she gets up and leaves.

Politely, I inquired as to why that was, and she responded, "I'm a Christian."

Again, very pleasantly, I asked what that meant regarding swear words.

She stated plainly, "It's not God's way."

I pointed out that if all language was created by God, wasn't the picking out of certain words to be defined as "naughty," or "bad," something man did?

She didn't answer, and instead turned away from me and started speaking to someone else.

I shrugged and went about my business, because that's all you can do. The exchange spoke to something I had to learn on my own, but that I tell you here: no matter how gentle you are, people do not like having their beliefs examined, or questioned.

I've just given you an example using religion, but the rule can be cast across a large swath of opinions, be they political, personal, artistic, or anything under the sun, really. Usually because people have beliefs without reason. It's just something they think, and they reason that's enough to make it right.

There's nothing wrong with belief, as long as it isn't rooted in anger or ignorance. Like racism, for example. To say you dislike an entire race or group of people because of their skin color or religion? There can be no justifying that. In the arena of art, however, if you like a movie or a song and someone else hates that movie or song? Big whoop. You like what you like, they like what they like, and such is life.

I have very few problems with anyone thinking almost anything. Sometimes I ask people why they believe what they believe because I'm interested; I'm curious as to why people think the way they think. So it disturbs and frightens me when they either cannot answer, or give an answer that is factually unsound.

By the way, I'm not trying to make the case religion is inherently bad, or even good, for that matter. There have been great religious leaders throughout history, most recently and notably, people like Bishop Desmond Tutu, the Dalai Lama, and Pope Francis. If someday you choose to follow a book written by goat herders who didn't know where the sun went at night, I will respect that the best I can, and hope that you do so because of spiritual men like them.

(Even though, no, the Dalai Lama isn't Christian. If you choose to be Buddhist, or Hindu, more power to you. Scientologist... well, then we're going to need to have a talk.)

I am planning on raising you to challenge and question everything, even and especially what I tell you. That said, you will have to be able to justify your beliefs. I'm not looking to change anyone, but I am open to the idea of changing myself.

When you're young, you'll think you know everything; when you're old, you'll realize you know nothing. Over the course of your life, you'll travel from arrogance to humility. It's an interesting and enlightening journey. For example, I was an atheist in high school. I didn't believe there was anything out there, and that death was the end of everything. Now I'm an adult, and I'm not sure what I believe. The best description is that I'm agnostic, otherwise known as someone too sissy to be an atheist. I think there might be some sort of universal power or energy out there, and I don't know what happens to people after they die.

These days my skepticism kicks in when someone says they know with certainty what that power (usually called "God") thinks, how it acts, what it wants, and how you need to behave in order to appease that power.

Mommy is somewhat the same; she doesn't follow any given religion, but she does believe in karma. The idea behind karma is "as you sow, so shall you reap," "do unto others," and myriad other ways of saying that what you put into the world is what you receive in return. Karma is an age-old concept, and it generally creates common ground when Venn diagramming religious and agnostic beliefs.

The thing is, while Mommy believes in karma, I do not. I believe life is random. Bad things happen to good people; great things happen to horrible people, and so on. Racists, homophobes, and rude people can be successful, while kind, loving, and talented people go hungry.

(And vice versa, of course. The odds aren't stacked just to favor bastards.)

Since I literally just said, "Be able to explain your beliefs," I will expand upon mine: I don't believe in karma because I personally know too many horrible people who are wildly successful, and at the same time have a few really talented friends who are wonderful people, yet struggle. It's as simple as that. Beyond that, I cannot look at a child going hungry and think either "It must be karma they're burning off from a previous lifetime," or "They must be burning off bad karma right now in order to have something good happen to them in the future." Neither makes sense, and thus I don't believe there is a give-and-take to how you act in life.

That doesn't give me (or anyone) an excuse to be a jerk, however. Just because there is no cause and effect to life does not give you the right to be ungrateful, or selfish. You act well toward others because it is the right thing to do, not because you expect rewards.

It's that simple.

The point of all this blathering on was supposed to be this: people don't like being questioned, even if innocently so. Most people find any sort of inquiry into their thought process to be an anathema.

Knowing that, you can decide what you want to do with the information. You can resolve to go with the flow and not ask questions, or you can ask questions knowing full well some people will respond poorly.

Love,

Dad

May 28

Hey Buddy...

I am in San Antonio, and after the early show tonight an elderly couple approached me. Somewhere in their eighties, they owned a pass that allowed them entry to any show that wasn't a special event.

They were very complimentary, and said they loved me and found my act hilarious. They explained that they use their pass to attend one show a week, and that they thought I was original, different, and that I should be a star.

I was quite flattered, to say the least. It warms me cockles when people who see a lot of comedy think I'm above and beyond what they're used to.

Because I mention being a father on stage, they asked about you and Sister. After answering, I, in turn, asked about their lives. It's the polite thing to do, but I fear it was a mistake in this case.

They grew quiet for a moment, and the smiles they had greeted me with left their faces. Then, in soft voices spoke of their only child, a son. He was a session musician, someone who played the drums for stars. Ray Charles was mentioned, but they said he played with many celebrity musicians, that he toured the world...

...and that he exited it too soon.

Their son died a little over ten years ago, and as the man talked about him a sad, faraway look crossed his wife's face.

"You never get over it. You never fully heal," she said softly.

After ten years, they still hadn't come to terms with the fact their child was gone.

I have to admit, it's probably my biggest fear—losing you or Sister. It would just... destroy me. I cannot fathom carrying on.

Parents should not outlive their children. If there is any rule in life, that should be the standard bearer.

Until you become a parent, the sentence is nothing more than a statement. You can read it, understand it, and agree with it. But you cannot feel it. You cannot understand the overwhelming emotions children bring out of you.

Before you and Sister were born, I thought I knew what love was. I thought I knew what love was during my first few relationships. I "loved" my first few girlfriends.

Then I met your mother, and it was a genuine light bulb moment.

"Oh! This is love."

The love I feel for your mother is different—better, deeper—than what I had felt with any woman before. I thought, "This is it. I get it now."

Then Sister, and then you, came along. It was like having my chest kicked wide open. The love I feel for you both simply eclipses all else. It is pervasive, all encompassing, and ever-present. The little nothings you both do, from flicking the light switch in your room on and off—something I listen to and smile as you put yourself to sleep and when you first wake up—to the way you pick out cereal in the morning.

146

(Your cereal, by the way, comes in two options: circles, or squares — Cheerios and Life, respectively. We keep a wide variety of Cheerios on hand, and every day Mommy or I run down the list for you: "Apple circles? Chocolate circles? Honey circles? Frosted? Fruity?" You shake your head and announce an adamant "No!" with every one you don't want. But when we get to your choice? You don't actually say yes. You laugh. You laugh like it's the funniest thing you've ever heard. Not because you think it's funny, mind you, but because you're expressing joy. Cereal makes you happy, and who are we to deny you happy?)

One thrill you discover upon becoming a parent is watching your child sleep; I watch you and Sister often.

You like sleeping with your door open; Sister likes hers mostly closed/slightly ajar. You both sleep under Christmas lights; yours blue, Sister's purple. They illuminate your respective rooms, and make it easy for middle-of-the-night spying. I'll awake for absolutely no reason — because my mind hates letting me get any amount of decent sleep — and decide to wander out into the living room. On the way, I pause at each of your doorways, ducking my head in to see what position you're each in.

(For the record, Sister generally sleeps on her side. But you? For some unknown [yet adorable] reason, you sleep on your belly, legs tucked in at the knees, booty square up in the air.)

No matter how often I check in on you, I never tire of it. I always marvel at how much just seeing you snooze peacefully explodes my heart.

It has been said that no matter how old your offspring gets, you always remember them as an infant. Whether at their first recital, or learning to drive, or going off to college... the parent sees a child, and wonders where the time went.

Speaking with the elderly couple tonight hurt. Thinking of them having to live with the ache of loss? It was rough. I hope that for a brief period of time, if even only a moment, I helped them forget their loss. Laughter is supposed to be healing, but I know that given their situation it was a Band-Aid on a gaping wound.

I will not forget them.

Love,

Dad

June 10

Hey Buddy...

I'm in Ottawa, Minnesota, right now. I dropped you and Sister off at daycare, exercised, and then drove up for the gig.

This morning at breakfast, the song "What I Got" by Sublime, came on. You immediately broke into a wide smile and started wiggle-dancing. Squirming in your chair, so happy from the sounds entering your wee little ears.

You've heard the song a few times, but this is the first time you treated it exactly like your favorite tune, "Roxanne." When that comes on, it's liquid listening gold.

I smiled at you, so you smiled even wider, so I wiggled, then you wiggled some more... we shared a little back-and-forth dance, and it was a wonderful moment.

It also made me somewhat reflective.

A friend posted a photo of Bradley Nowell — the former singer of Sublime — online recently; she was pausing to reflect on Bradley's death many years ago.

I found the picture difficult to view.

In the photo, Bradley is sitting on a couch, holding his infant son Jakob in one arm, and a guitar in the other. Next to them is Bradley's famous Dalmatian, Louie.

Jakob is staring up at Bradley like infants do; wide-eyed to the world around them, somewhat confused to be alive. Louie is lovingly enthralled by his adopted, human father, as he always was.

(Louie and Bradley went everywhere together.)

The picture is heartbreaking, because all I could see was a man who threw away fatherhood, for fucking heroin.

If I examine my response, I think the emotions I am mired in come about due to the fact Nowell exited the child's life so quickly into his existence; Jakob was only eleven months old when he lost his father. I find that offensive, and can't really muster up the ability to care that I'm being a judgmental prick for being offended.

A baby knows two things: love, and pain. When your infant is in pain, you want nothing more than to end the suffering, to absorb whatever is making it unwell. When emitting love, the rest of the world fades away and all that matters are the eyes staring at you in wonder. So while I understand, logically, that addiction is a difficult demon to challenge, my sympathy ends there. I bring too much emotion to the table to be forgiving.

You stare at me in a manner not unlike Jakob eyeing Bradley. When I enter your room in the morning, your arms reach out— "Pick me up, Daddy, I want to be held." When I return from a week on the road, upon seeing me or hearing my voice, your little face lights up with a huge, partially-toothy smile. It radiates warmth, joy, and innocence.

I observe the world through a different lens these days; what I see involves empathy for anyone participating in the marathon called parenthood. We live in a violent, unfair world, and the best some of us can do is provide love for our children. Whatever challenges are provided by circumstance, you fight them with everything you have, no question. Succumbing to drugs seems too easy a cop out by comparison.

Of course, maybe leaving the child to be raised by others is for the best. I mean, would it be better to never know your father, or to live with one who is an addict? Arguments could be made both ways, I suppose, but I cannot help but think that in the least you should give your child a chance to get sick of you.

As always, if I am judging others I must pause and scrutinize my own hypocrisies. I drive extensively for a living. Considering "traffic fatality" is an extremely high-risk way of shuffling off this mortal coil, am I selfish, too? Would it be better for you if I locked myself into a 9-to-5 job, one more safe than dodging big rig drivers bug-eyed on homemade amphetamines break necking it to their destination because the boys are thirsty in Atlanta?

I don't know, I don't know, I don't know. All I understand is: my heart lives inside you and your sister. It is that simple.

No flowery prose is required to describe the love I feel for you. You and your sister are twin suns that I orbit. I hope to never do anything so selfish that will remove one minute I can spend with the two of you as your father.

Because, to put it in the words of a talented poet: "Lovin'... is what I got."

Love,

Dad

June 15

Hey Buddy…

I was twelve when I first learned about homosexuality.

My family was on vacation in Provincetown, Massachusetts; we were visiting my uncles, Joel and Ray. The thing is, only Joel was a blood relation to my father.

In Provincetown, a Gay Mecca during the summer months, I saw men holding hands with men and women holding hands with women. Suddenly the idea both Joel and Ray were my dad's brother didn't hold much weight.

So, homosexuality was explained to me, and that was that. I shrugged, and everyone went on with their life.

Children are basically open-minded sponges waiting to be told what to think of the world around them. Since no one was telling me to stare, hate, or feel uncomfortable in Provincetown, I quickly surmised everything must be OK. The situation didn't seem to be doing anyone or anything any harm—it was just people acting in a way I wasn't overly familiar with.

Everywhere I looked, I saw acceptance. No one stared, no one judged, no one pointed fingers or accused. Everyone walked around as if the situation were entirely normal.

Which, in Provincetown, it was.

Which, in life, it should be.

Cut to my adult life.

I have a very stupid... I guess I'll call him "friend," although "acquaintance" or "someone I tolerate" might be more appropriate. Without getting into specifics, we were discussing different lifestyles, which caused him to get quite angry and ask, "What if my son sees some man wearing a dress? How am I supposed to explain that?"

All I could think was, "Did you have to explain the first black person they saw?"

If he did, I imagine the conversation would be, "Well, some people are white, some are black, and there are a multitude of ethnicities across the planet."

Or, to take that one further: some men wear dresses. Big whoop. Most men wear pants, some wear dresses. Some men like men, most men like women. Some women like women, some people like vanilla, others like chocolate...

It really is that simple. Prejudice has to be taught; it is not an inherent condition.

Which means my stupid friend was exposing his own insecurities, not actually worrying about his child.

Which brings me to the point of this letter. Several days ago, a man named Omar Mateen went to a dance club in Orlando, Florida—a dance club specifically for homosexual men. Gay bars and dance clubs act as refuge from the world around them—a safe haven where gay men and women can relax, be themselves, and not have to worry about the many people in America who believe their very existence is inappropriate.

Omar entered the club armed with two guns, and opened fire. He murdered forty-nine people and injured at least fifty-three others before being shot and killed by the police.

For the past several days, everyone has been talking about gun control, a terrorist group called ISIS, homophobia, and radical Islam.

Yet no one is talking about Omar Mateen's parents.

It's becoming fairly obvious Omar was a closeted homosexual, someone who couldn't find acceptance at home or in his community. As one of my friends put it, "It was easier for him to be branded a member of ISIS, than gay."

In fact, Omar's father, Mir Seddique, said in an interview: "Omar saw two men kissing and got very angry."

The only thing that would fuel such anger is a lifetime of being told it is wrong to be homosexual, and that comes from upbringing. It could come from religion, or general familial intolerance.

So what made Omar angry about two men kissing? The fact they were comfortable enough to express their love freely while he could not? Maybe a fantasy that they were accepted by their families, where he would not be? The knowledge he couldn't go to his father, Mir Seddique Mateen, and discuss his true sexual orientation with him?

While those questions are speculation, there is absolutely a direct connection between homophobia and Omar's childhood. As stated, children are not inherently bigoted; it has to be taught. Omar was raised under a roof of prejudice. In the same interview where he mentioned Omar's anger over kissing men, his father

155

stated: "God himself will punish those involved in homosexuality, this is not for the servants."

That is a frightening, and telling, quote.

You cannot prevent children from hearing racial or homophobic slurs, but you can teach them to understand how hateful they are. That is my duty to you, and Sister. You will be raised to love people no matter their race, religion, or orientation.

If he had been brought up on a foundation of acceptance, Omar wouldn't have been filled with self-loathing. He wouldn't have been a clear-cut example of "We hate in others what we see in ourselves."

If Omar's parents had told him, "We will love you no matter who you love," forty-nine innocent people would still be alive.

I will love you, and Sister, no matter who you love.

Love,

Dad

June 18

Hey Buddy...

Several days ago, a young boy roughly your age (as I write this) died a horrible death.

(Great way to open a letter, I know.)

Lane Graves was with his family, visiting Disney World in Florida. He was splashing at the edge of a man-made lagoon when an alligator popped out of nowhere and dragged him underwater.

Reading about it made me almost throw up. I literally, not figuratively but literally, felt a sickness in my stomach. It wasn't just the fact something so horrible happened to a child, but the fact he was similar to you in age that made it hit so hard.

I have a picture of you hugging a teddy bear you got for Christmas. Your face is beaming as you hold it tight, both your arms are wrapped around the bear, pressing every inch of it against your little body in a moment of pure love and enjoyment.

That image of you with your teddy bear seared into my mind as I read of Lane's fate.

Then I entered a very dark place.

I wondered what was going through Lane's mind as the alligator grabbed him. How confused and scared he must have been as it dragged him underwater, wanting only his mother or father, wondering where they were, not knowing what was happening, knowing only terror and pain...

That's when I started crying.

I felt horrible for Lane's parents, understanding their anguish must be insurmountable. I didn't lash out, asking in anger "Where were they?" or shout "It was their fault!"

But others did.

After every tragedy, the Internet is where people express empathy, understanding, and unfortunately, ignorance and anger.

A child fell into a gorilla pen at a zoo in Cincinnati. Zookeepers had to shoot the gorilla to get the child out, and people yelled, "How dare they shoot the gorilla! It's the parents fault the kid was in there!" No thought was given to the structure or how unsafe it must have been to allow a toddler access.

The gay nightclub that got shot up in Orlando, the one mentioned in my previous letter? Right after that happened, a homophobic pastor in California, a supposed man of God, told his congregation: "I'm kind of upset [the shooter] didn't finish the job."

After Lane died, indignant and awful people shouted, "There were signs that said 'No Swimming'!"

If you spend any time online, you'd think humanity is at its nadir. People revel in self-righteous attitudes as they mock or belittle tragedy. Reading the spiteful attacks had me concerned about the path humanity was on, but then I remembered a stop I once made in Ohio.

While traveling for work, I visited Kent State University.

I had passed it several times, and finally decided that, considering the significance it played in American history—a deadly protest took place here during the Vietnam War—I should pay my respects.

After locating the memorial, I did the walking tour, pausing at each plaque to read the name of the fallen student.

It was sobering.

It was to my surprise, then, when I watched a documentary on the massacre and discovered that at the time, support was behind the National Guard. Students were looked upon as dirty hippies, and good Americans believed in president Nixon and his war. In fact, following the shooting a Gallup poll revealed that 58% of respondents blamed the students for what happened. Only 11% said responsibility lay with the National Guard.

In other words, had the Internet existed, "They had it coming" would have made up the majority of any comments section. People believed that students exercising their First Amendment right to assemble and giving voice to their freedom of speech were at fault for being shot.

Reflecting on that, I started thinking about current tragedies in a new way, one that sent me down a historical path.

America was founded by a population who thought slaughtering indigenous people was acceptable. Following that, slavery was the societal norm, and once that ended segregation was hunky-dory. Between the end of slavery and desegregation, child labor, profound sexism and female marginalization were all widespread and popular. In fact, the outliers who challenged slavery, segregation, child labor, or sexism were attacked for defying the system.

Using this lens of historical sins, witnessing a segment of modern society react inappropriately to a family losing their child suddenly makes sense. It's not that humanity is doomed, or that people are becoming more selfish — the sad truth is that we've always been like this.

The difference is the Internet.

The Internet gives everyone a voice, so now we are more aware of those without compassion. While I believe there are more loving voices out there than angry ones, the self-righteous, furious ones stay with us longer. It is more upsetting to see someone attack a family who just lost a child than it is to read tender words of support. The angry words make you livid, and anger takes time to recover from.

Fortunately, reactions and perspective have a way of changing with time and enlightenment.

Today, the Kent State Massacre is looked upon with reverence, not indifference.

As details came out regarding the Cincinnati Zoo, it was revealed the exhibit has an open-faced gorilla pen for a better viewing experience. Of course a four-year-old could make his way inside; it was a dangerous set up.

(My friend Jake said, "If you own a zoo, once a month you should have to actively try to get a four-year-old in with the animals. If you succeed, the zoo isn't safe enough and you have to shut it down.")

Several days after the tragedy in Florida, a mother posted pictures online of her son standing in the same spot that Lane was taken by the alligator. He was standing in less than 6 inches of water, and the photo had been taken a mere 30 minutes before Lane's family arrived. No one was swimming, and there were no signs warning, "HEY!!! DEADLY ALLIGATORS LIVE HERE!"

(Even worse, several days after the heartbreak, stories popped up of visitors feeding alligators in that very lagoon, meaning Disney knew there was an alligator problem. Then a video surfaced of an alligator next to Splash Mountain, meaning they were an ongoing and ignored issue. What happened to Lane was not due to negligent parenting, as awful people tried to say.)

In California, 1,000 protesters shouted "love conquers hate" at the homophobic pastor Roger Jimenez, showing his message was only finding a home among the most awful people, not the masses.

People may be quick to rush to judgment, but with more information, sometimes they come around.

Maybe next time they will offer condolences first, and wait for all the facts to come in before pointing fingers of accusation.

There will always be those who feel compassion toward others in times of tragedy, and those who feel self-righteous.

But it's no worse than it's ever been.

Written to you from Duluth, Minnesota.

Love,

Dad

June 25

Hey Buddy...

I am in Dubuque, Iowa.

There is no way to ease into things, so I will state outright that this letter is going to be rough, and messy.

A few weeks ago, an event in California rocked the country. Since then, I've been trying to digest what happened — to come to terms with the planet we live on in order to help guide you as a person.

A young man in California raped a young woman and was then given the lightest prison sentence possible as punishment. The judge failed in his duty to protect women from sexual predators, and instead worried about the consequences the man might face having an assault charge on his record.

Read that again, if you have to.

The judge put the needs of a rapist above those of his victim and society as a whole. The judge failed to hand down requisite punishment, which both failed to protect women from this individual rapist, but also sent a horrific message to other sexual predators: what you're doing isn't so bad. Go ahead. If you're caught, you'll get a slap on the wrist.

The man was convicted of rape; let there be no confusion. He was arrested, tried, and found guilty. Which means he should have gone to prison for many years. When you inflict violence upon another person, you should be removed from civilization. During the course of sentencing deliberation, however, the rapist's father wrote a letter asking for clemency. The father said his poor little boy would be forever damaged by the verdict, which was punishment enough for his actions.

I am outraged and disgusted by the lack of punishment, and more so by the actions of that man's father. That father failed his son.

There was no thought in the rapist's head telling him what he was doing was wrong. There was no parental figure, no voice of authority, no moral compass that prevented him from damaging another human being. The fact that father was worried more about his son's punishment than his son's victim shows you exactly what kind of person we're dealing with. In order to be a complete human being you need empathy. You need a sense of right and wrong, and the ability to square your shoulders and accept responsibility for your actions. You need to be the exact opposite of the rapist, and his father.

Let me tell you a story.

I haven't thought of this in... God, probably fifteen years. Some of the details have been lost in the gray matter of my mind, but the important actions remain.

I was in my twenties, probably about the same age as the rapist I've been talking about. I was driving to a friend's house. It was autumn—October or November—it was late at night, and it was cold. I was on a rural road, out in the middle of proverbial nowhere, when I came across a teenage girl walking on the side of the road. She wasn't wearing a coat, and had her arms wrapped around herself trying to maintain a sense of warmth.

I immediately pulled over and asked if she needed a ride. She was drunk, and happily hopped into my car.

Her house was a ten-minute drive — which would have been a hell of a walk — and during our trip she explained that she had gotten into a fight with her boyfriend at a party and stormed off.

I got her home; she said "Thanks" and stumbled inside.

And that was that.

While my exterior was calm, from the moment I saw her until the moment she exited my car, the only thought screaming inside my head was: What if it wasn't ME that had driven by?

What if someone horrible had driven by? What if someone who had evil thoughts had picked her up? She got in the first car door that opened, and it worked out well for her. If someone awful had scooped her up, that girl would have become what is known as a "statistic." Even though I am not religious by any means, the thought thank God I came across her first remained inside my mind for several hours after the event.

I bring this up, because in life, you will be presented with situations. Maybe a girl you like will get drunk and pass out in your bed. Maybe you'll attain a position of power where you can take advantage of people. Maybe you'll come across someone incapacitated and in need of a ride home.

In those situations, you will be defined as a person. Will you act honorably, or will you do harm?

It never crossed my mind to take advantage of that girl. Is it because of how I'm wired, or my upbringing? I don't know. I don't know what makes one person normal and another awful. I never got a talking to about how to treat women; I never got a sex talk from my parents, and I don't remember when I learned what rape was. I think that according to societal norms back then, it was something you didn't talk about. It was just assumed that you don't assault, hurt, or rape women.

There are those who like to glorify the past—to create a false narrative of what was, and shout, "Back in my day, we didn't have to discuss rape. We didn't do things like that."

Not true.

It's specifically because of the lack of dialogue that rape occurs, and we can no longer continue down the path of silence. It is in silence we allow problems to fester and actions to continue.

So.

Here we are.

I am a father, and you are my son. It falls square on my shoulders to educate you. The only way to end rape is to raise good boys that become good men. As you are only two years old, I envision you growing up to be a young man with morals. But I know it's my job to instill ethics in you, not just assume that you will understand non-consensual sex is wrong. I have to lay it out for you.

No means no.

That might read as overly simple, but it's a solid truth. There is no way around it. If a woman says "Stop," you stop. It doesn't matter how far along you are in a relationship or even the process. If you are in the middle of consensual sex and she changes her mind and says "Stop," you pull out. End of discussion. If you put your arm around her and she says "No," you stop. End of discussion. "No" and "Stop" are to be taken at face value; there are no variables here. Also: if someone is incoherent—too drunk or on drugs—they cannot give consent.

Look, this might seem intimidating, and possibly scary. Maybe it should be. I don't know. People like absolutes, and I wish I had every answer. But I don't. And there's nothing I can do about that.

I don't want you to enter into the world of dating full of fear; I don't want you to hold back from having fun because you have my nagging voice inside your head every time you talk to a girl.

But I know that every rapist had one thing in common: a father that failed him.

I will not fail you.

Love,

Dad

July 6

Hey Buddy…

A milestone occurred today.

We are in Madison, Wisconsin, visiting Graw Janet and Bada Joe. Today at nap you discovered how to climb out of your Pack 'n Play.

I put you down, and several minutes later you were banging on the bedroom door, wanting out.

Mommy and I were stunned. Mommy put you back to bed, and you popped right back out.

Then it was my turn.

This continued several more times, until finally Mommy had to go nap with you just to keep you in bed.

Tonight, then, the Pack 'n Play out of the question, we decided to let you sleep on the air mattress with Sister.

And holy poop on a stick, you two went to bed holding hands.

It was the most heartwarming thing Mommy and I have ever seen.

Sleep to you rarely comes easy; when it's time for bed you want nothing to do with it. You know there's so much more going on in the world that you need to examine.

You have discovered the switches on the wall above your crib. One starts the fan spinning, which you enjoy; the other flicks the light on and off, much to your amusement.

Because you have figured out the light switch, after Mommy or I leave you, you immediately flip the light on and begin "reading" whatever book you have with you. Because you always have a book in the crib with you. Yes, there are the requisite stuffed animals, but as you are put into the crib, you always intone, "Book!"

That is your security blanket; the thing most dear to you. A book. Any book. When given one, you pull it tightly to your body and snuggle in and ready yourself for sleep.

When you wake, it's right there next to you, and you flip through the pages, calling out the letters you recognize (all 26 of them), and pointing at any picture you recognize.

"Fire truck!" "Lion!" "Doggie!"

When I enter, you smile and hand me the book, then raise your arms so I can lift you out.

Sometimes the dog comes in to sniff around, and you point and shout, "Doggie!"

Seeing him always puts a smile on your face.

From there, you have a routine.

I set you down, and because you are awake before your sister 99% of the time, you go looking for her.

As you have not yet mastered the art of turning door knobs, you go to her room and push on her door; if it was left open a crack overnight, you enter freely. If it was closed, you stand there, frustrated, pushing ever harder and flailing away at the knob.

I open the door for you, and you scurry inside and then scramble onto your sister's bed.

She half-wakes as you lie down right atop her, your arms around her, snuggling in for hugs.

Which your sister gives you in her sleep.

The instant your little head touches her chest, whichever arm of hers is free—because one hand is always occupied via thumb-in-mouth—wraps around you and pulls you in tight.

The two of you will probably fight fierce battles over toys and other nonsense in future years, but for right now you adore one another.

It is nothing short of incredible.

Love,

Dad

July 22

Hey Buddy…

I am in Royal Oak, Michigan.

A few letters ago, I told you that I am agnostic. I believe there's something out there, I'm just not sure what.

I have enough mental clarity to see that all religions are as manmade as a refrigerator or automobile, but I can't bring myself to go full-blown atheist.

Why? Because every so often I get a nudge, a reminder that says, "Hey, keep that ego of yours in check."

Some would dismiss it as happenstance; some would call it the hand of God.

I'm not sure what to think.

But I notice.

*   *   *

It is New Year's Eve, with 1998 breathing its dying gasp and 1999 crowning like a baby's head. I am in a small, sparsely attended dive bar with my friend Troy. We are here because Troy is a good person.

I will soon betray him.

Seven weeks earlier, five days before my birthday, in fact, the first woman I loved decided she didn't want me in her life anymore. Silly me, I thought I would spend the rest of my life with her.

Actually, she — Judy — made the decision to end things long before informing me. She just needed to figure out a few things first, such as, "Will the guy I cheated on Nathan with be my boyfriend now?"

(You don't let go of one vine until the next is in your hand, right?)

I haven't talked to her since the next day, when I dropped off a box of mementos: a locket of hair she had given me, a postcard featuring Man o' War she sent me while traveling, movie tickets from our first date...

(My lord, I have remembrances of yours that I have longèd to redeliver. I pray you now receive them.)

Judy and I met at a restaurant where we once worked. That means most of our friends are former coworkers. On this 1998 New Year's Eve, Judy is hosting a party with her new boyfriend. All our mutual friends are at the party except for Troy; he is kind enough to hang with me, the uninvited.

We are having the discussions people have when one is in the throes of depression and the other is a comforting soul, me saying, "I don't understand the treachery," and Troy assuring me, "I don't get it. You're much better than the new guy."

There is a lag in the conversation, because you can only beat those same thoughts into the ground so often.

Our silence hangs in the air a moment, a question mark suspended atop it wondering which of us will break it, when "Train in Vain" starts playing on the jukebox.

The question mark disappears, and an unspoken understanding takes place between us; neither will interrupt the song. Me because I'm reveling in the pain and free-form association, Troy because he is (most likely) tired of my blathering.

The song finishes. Troy and I have not said a word for three minutes and nine seconds. As it fades into the next arrangement, Troy says, "Wow. That was like... perfect."

It was.

As I am unable to make sense of my life, I stand and walk out into the night. I have not grabbed my coat, because I don't need it. Troy follows, as he is worried about my state of mind.

Standing in the cold—records say it was five degrees—I feel nothing. I strip off my shirt and absorb the winter air into my skin. Troy looks on in worry, wondering what this idiot friend of his is up to. He tries to get me to put my jacket on, but I decline. I just stand in the cold, breathing in, breathing out.

I'm trying to feel something other than numb, or maybe I'm trying to numb my body so it distracts me from the emotion overpowering me.

I take my leave of Troy; I need to be alone. He goes to Judy's party, and I'm fine with that. He's sacrificed enough of his holiday for me.

I will spend the next two years of my life seeing a therapist.

*   *   *

It is March 14, 2015, and I am driving through my old neighborhood.

I'm performing in Milwaukee and have a lunch date with a good friend. There's a Thai restaurant from my college days I love, one with a dish I've been unable to find anywhere else. That the restaurant has remained in business all these years, with that item still front and center, should tell you how special it is.

As I near my old apartment, a wry smile of nostalgia crosses my face. I pull up to a stop sign and glance my left, right, and left again when my memory kicks in.

The bar.

I haven't thought of it in over a decade, but there it is.

The memories of that New Year's Eve spark in me, and as they do "Train in Vain" comes on my radio.

The hair on my arms raise a little.

I am neither upset nor alarmed, but more... Keanu Reeves.

Whoa.

My smile widens, and becomes more grateful than wry. Though the moment has taken me by surprise, I have already been down this emotional path. It was an incredibly dark period of my life, one of deep pain. When you give your heart and soul to someone and they tell you those items hold no value, it attacks your self-worth.

I became a very bitter person for a while, but eventually worked through it all. Now I look back on it as one of the best things to ever happen to me. Had I not been dumped, I wouldn't have eventually met the woman I married, and I wouldn't have the two children I love more than life itself. Had I not learned the pain of infidelity, I might not be the loyal mate I am today.

Not long after that New Year's Eve I cut off ties with anyone "stuck in the middle" between Judy and me. I didn't want to force an ultimatum on anyone, but couldn't be around them; I couldn't be reminded of her constantly if I was to ever heal. Troy was a good person, but I couldn't handle the knowledge that on Monday he was hanging out with me, and on Tuesday, Judy. Maybe saying I betrayed him was a little too harsh, but I know he was surprised and possibly angered by my decision to walk away from our friendship.

Though I hold no regrets for my actions, now that they're so far in the rearview I almost wonder what it would be like to talk to Troy, or any of the other friends I shared with Judy back then.

To return to the beginning of this thought process, some might call that precise song playing at that precise moment so many years later the hand of God. Others would call it random.

As I relived a memory that hadn't fired across my synapses in years, thinking thoughts of appreciation for all I went through, all I could think was:

D: It is written.

I just don't know who the author is.

I tell you all this so that when you are at your darkest moments, facing either heartbreak or rejection of another kind, you have to focus on the idea: everything happens for a reason.

Sometimes that will be the only thing keeping you sane.

Love,

Dad

July 26

Hey Buddy...

A few weeks ago I was in San Antonio, Texas. I wrote to you about a couple I met while there, but while farting around online I was reminded of my first trip to the city.

As a rule, I generally don't give money to panhandlers. I will donate food to a pantry or money to a charity, but I don't give directly to people. It's the age-old adage, the one about giving a man a fish versus buying him cable so he can watch the fishing channel.

Or something like that.

While in San Antonio, in line at a little Mexican restaurant, however, I did a one-eighty on my standard operating procedure.

I didn't know the city or the restaurant; I had been driving, saw the place, suddenly realized I hadn't eaten in seven hours, and pulled over. Wandering in and examining the overhead menu, I figured it was worth staying, so I got in line. Fairly soon after I arrived, a homeless man arrived and stood behind me. I didn't think anything of it, until he got out his money.

He had one dollar. One dollar, and some change.

I saw him look at the menu, and then down at the change in his hand. As he counted through it — the change in one palm and the index finger on his other hand shuffling through it for accuracy —

179

I was asked to order. I picked a $5 enchilada platter. I got out my wallet and paid, and then looked at the homeless man.

"Hey," I said. "You got enough there to get what you need?"

He was either startled or embarrassed, because he answered so quietly it was barely audible. "I think so. Thank you."

I nodded and went and found a table to wait for my number to be called. The man collected a soda cup, filled it with iced tea and took a table on the other side of the restaurant.

My number was shouted out; I went up to collect my food. While returning to my table, I heard a gentle voice say, "Excuse me."

I turned to see the man looking at me with sad eyes.

"Does your offer still stand?" he asked politely.

"Absolutely," I said, reaching for my wallet.

"I was only thirsty when I ordered," he explained, "but I should probably eat."

I gave him a couple of bucks, he thanked me, and I returned to my table and stared at my food.

Though I had entered somewhat ravenous, I was immediately completely uninterested in my meal. I picked at it a little, then decided I had to leave; I no longer felt like eating. I didn't want to be there, I wasn't hungry, and something was wrong inside me.

I got up and walked my tray over to his table, and where I had ordered the enchilada platter, he had a simple, small bowl of

Spanish rice in front of him. It was without doubt the cheapest item on the menu.

I set my tray down, "I didn't really touch this," I said. "I filled up pretty quickly."

He looked up at me with his sad eyes, thanked me with his shy, soft voice, and I left.

I got into my car, pulled out my expensive and seemingly self-indulgent phone, and emailed Mommy. I told her what happened, and that for reasons I didn't understand, I felt awful. She did her best to cheer me up; her warm words filling a cold screen, trying to assuage my first-world guilt.

Safe in the cocoon of my car, reading "Why do you feel bad? You did a good thing!" I teared up and began to cry. It wasn't sobbing, the tears just trickled out of me, an uncontrolled sadness doing its best to escape my guilt-ridden body.

I don't really know why I felt so horrible, but the thoughts going through my head were: Should I have just offered to pay for his lunch while I was paying for mine? Did I give him enough money? What was he going to do for dinner?

Why didn't I do more?

The last question is the one that haunted me.

I didn't know anything about this man, or his history. He may have beaten his wife and kids at one time; he may have had a great job but abused alcohol or drugs and wasted away his fortunes and talents. I had no clue, and I didn't care. In the moment I saw him, in that one moment he was counting the change in his hand to see if he could afford to feed himself, all I saw was a fragile human in need. A man searching for the most basic of all needs: sustenance. And that moment hit me in places I don't like to admit exist.

My tears only lasted about twenty seconds, and a mere ten minutes later I was swearing at my GPS for taking me to a residential neighborhood and telling me I was at the car wash I was looking for.

You have moments in life that reach the core of who you are supposed to be and how you are supposed to think, and then they fade. Just like that I was back in the safe world of blinders and apathy.

I'd like to pretend that a moment like that changes a person, but I think it's just a bump in the road, a momentary shift of consciousness. A bump where it is knocked into us how lucky we are. The very next day, we are somehow left wanting. Our computer isn't powerful enough, our television isn't big enough... somehow our magnificent life pales next to the life we see in advertisements, where everyone is pretty, and everyone is happy.

How soon we forget.

Hopefully you will remember to be a better all-around person than your father is.

Love,

Dad

August 7

Hey Buddy…

You don't know this yet, but you sleep like me. Your sister sleeps like Mommy. By that I mean that nothing short of an earthquake during the storming of Normandy wakes those two, while a butterfly fart two miles from our house startles us out of a slumber. Also, the women under our roof can fall asleep at the drop of a hat on a bed of rocks. You and I struggle, and memorize ceilings instead of snoozing.

To that end, we are currently at Aunt Kayla's house. Mommy's mom—Graw Diane, as you know her—is getting married tomorrow, and we are spending the weekend here. Last night at your bedtime—which is several hours earlier than when the adults turn in—Mommy said, "I'm going to lay in bed with Truman until he falls asleep."

I was sitting outside the room in one of Aunt Kayla's recliners, farting around online and possibly doing some writing. Ten minutes went by before I heard the bedroom door creak open.

I didn't think anything of it; I figured Mommy was sneaking out and headed back upstairs to continue visiting with her sisters. Moments later, however, your little hand touched my arm. I looked at you, and you smiled.

I laughed and got up, and you immediately darted back into the bedroom. I hadn't said a word, but you knew you weren't supposed to be out carousing. I followed you, and there was Mommy, asleep on the bed. She had dozed off first, leaving you to your own devices. After glancing back to make sure I was still enforcing the rules, you snuggled in next to her. I returned to my computer.

Less than twenty seconds later, you were back at my side. I shooed you away, and this pattern then repeated itself a half-dozen times. By your third excursion I didn't even have to get up; when I heard the door, I would turn and give you a mock-dramatic look, and you would giggle and dart back into the bedroom. A couple of seconds later, however, you'd be back out, waiting to get chased back in. It was obviously a game; how fast can Daddy catch me?

You're becoming such an aware little toddler now that you're bumping up against age two. Just the idea that you knew you were supposed to be in bed when I started to get up the first time — somewhere in you, you realized you were being "naughty" and that I was going to shoo you away.

There are other signs your comprehension levels are increasing. This morning, Mommy said: "Go upstairs, we're going to the park," and you immediately bee-lined it to the stairs and crawl-climbed up them.

That may sound like nothing to you, but to me it was a clear case of absolute understanding. Mommy said "Go upstairs," and to the stairs you went.

The most enjoyable slice of parenting is watching babies become toddlers, and toddlers become tykes. The little moments — you knowing what stairs are, and climbing them upon command; watching you examine the world around you and try to make sense of it — those little moments boggle my Daddy mind.

I cannot wait to discover what you do next.

Love,

Dad

August 14

"Sometimes I feel like, I'm so uninvited, like something so out of touch. They tell me depression runs in the family, well that doesn't help me much."

~Todd Snider

Hey Buddy...

I am in Bloomington, Illinois tonight, and I'm thinking about the first comedy show I ever attended.

Mommy likes to joke that I have no soul, because I don't cry. She, for the record, weeps at the drop of a hat: during movies, a commercial, while reading... She even cried at the birth of both you and Sister, and seriously, who does that?

(What, everyone does? My bad.)

Mom is quite in tune with her sad side, because she suffers from clinical depression. She was diagnosed and placed on medication at age twenty and it changed her world. For the first time since childhood, evil thoughts weren't pounding away at her constantly, making her feel worthless, or that her life had no value.

I've never been diagnosed as manic-depressive, but it's prevalent on my father's side of the family, and I have had plenty of damaging thoughts about my self-worth.

I have also been right on the cusp of suicide.

My story is no secret, and it is neither original nor special. I moved a lot as a child, and my parents had an unhappy marriage. Combine those two and you have a kid who thinks friendships don't last and love isn't real. I swam inside the idea I would never have friends, or be loved. Once beliefs like that are ingrained in your cellular structure, they live with you for decades. You can combat the feelings using positive influences such as therapy or medication, or you can self-medicate with drugs, alcohol, or, my method of choice: comedy.

(Everyone knows you don't become a comedian when everything is right inside your noggin.)

Again, this was wasn't an original reaction to what I felt; most comics worth their salt have something hidden inside that pushes them to the spotlight. Personally, comedy was both a weapon and a shield. It became an armament that gave me distance from the world — think Pink Floyd's *The Wall* — and was a weapon used to attack when feeling defensive.

(Which, to someone depressed, is quite often.)

Like any drug, you eventually build up an immunity to it. For a while, the glory of a great show sits with you and carries you through the dark hours. But after a while, it's not enough. As a comedian, you go from being on stage in front of two hundred people, basking in the glory of their laughter...

...to alone in your hotel room, the thoughts of worthlessness screaming at you at the top of their lungs.

So, when your main drug fails, you combine it with others; the alone gets shut out using women, alcohol, pot, and whatever you can get your hands on.

My drugs during bouts of depression were music, and anger. Music, because there were songs I could relate to and not feel so alone in the world. No matter what I was going through, I could tether to an artist and understand I was neither unique nor special. They knew what I was going through, which mattered to me.

Anger, because when I was at my wits end and absolutely ready to end it all, the overwhelming desire to say "Fuck you!" to whatever higher power may be out there — God? — would carry me through. Sadness happens, so buck up and deal with it ya pansy. Every fiber of my body would be telling me to do it, just exit this world to escape the pain, but suicide seemed like losing. And I hate losing.

*   *   *

Mork & Mindy was a TV show that premiered in 1978.

I was eight years old.

In life, that's what's known as "perfect timing," as the show was aimed directly at eight-year-old sensibilities. I had no clue who Robin Williams was; I just knew that I laughed at the wacky man pretending to be an alien.

I more than laughed, actually. I reflected. Each episode ended with a moral, an oft-times touching moment where Mork waxed philosophic on what he was learning on Earth, and reported that information to Orson. It was in those moments I discovered the genius that was Robin Williams; he could make you laugh, but he wanted to make you cry.

(Maybe because if you were crying, he felt not so alone in his pain. I cannot say that with absolute certainty, but I don't believe it's too far a throw.)

An instant fan, I became obsessed with both Robin, and Mork. I scampered around the house saying "Nanu-nanu" and "Shazbot." I begged and was taken to The World According to Garp, a movie not exactly marketed to a twelve year old. Good Morning Vietnam made me howl; Dead Poets Society choked me up.

Robin Williams was also the first stand-up comedian I saw live.

I would have been... I can't remember. Sixteen or seventeen. He was performing at the Riverside Theater in Milwaukee, and when I heard about the show I immediately called for tickets. Naturally, the show was sold out, but they were considering adding a second performance; did I want to be on a waiting list?

Hell to the yeah I did.

A late show was added, and I got my tickets. I remember absolutely nothing of the evening, save for the fact I missed over half the jokes because I was still laughing at the one before. Tears ran down my face, and my face and jaw hurt at the end of the night.

To me, Robin Williams was a god. He meant more to me than just about everyone.

(Except Martin Riggs. Long story. Your dad is an oddball.)

Robin was open about two of his drugs—alcohol and cocaine—but I've not heard anyone discuss his other weaknesses: women, and marriage. Comedians aren't special creatures; like anyone else, they find solace in the arms of a lover to assuage the hole in their life.

Robin Williams cheated on one wife, married his daughter's nanny, and then married a third woman just a few years outside the end of his near-21-year second marriage. I will neither judge nor analyze his behavior, but I will say I am all too familiar with the pattern: the thoughts of not wanting to be alone, and of wanting to feel loved when you believe you're unlovable. In my younger years, I entered into several relationships too quickly, if only because I was astounded by the fact someone seemed to like me.

"This one is fooled," I would think. "Better not let her go!"

It was only when I reached my mid-30s that the desperation faded; I went through therapy and examined the origins of my insecurities, and hit my Malcolm Gladwell tipping point of failed relationships. I began to attack my depression, and eventually realized what I had wasn't medical; I didn't have a disease, I just had a shitty childhood I needed to deal with.

Thankfully.

Unlike me, Robin Williams suffered from manic depression. That means his hole was larger than most, one that couldn't be filled by millions of dollars or awards. When he looked in the mirror he didn't see an icon — he saw his own insecurities.

And in the end, that was too much to bear.

After his death, arguments aplenty littered the Internet. Did he kill himself, or end his own pain? Was his act selfish, or was it his choice to make?

I don't care.

I just know what his death meant to me.

On August 11, 2014, I was at the gym when the news broke. I had just finished up my workout, grabbed my phone, and a text was waiting for me: "Robin Williams, dead. Suicide."

I think my only surprise was at how not surprised I was. Knowing his life and story… I don't want to say I expected it, but after Belushi, Farley, Jeni, and Geraldo… It just wasn't as out of left field for me as it may have been for others.

But that didn't make it any less tragic.

As I drove home, I started to well up. Pulling into the garage, I could feel the tears behind my eyes. I got out of my car and opened the door to our house; inside, Sister, two years old at the time, was playing on the floor in the kitchen.

"Daddy!" she shouted happily.

"Hi sweety," I croaked, and became self-conscious. It was really going to happen.

Mommy asked me something and I tried answering, and she heard it in my voice. Alarmed, she jumped up, saw my eyes, and started peppering me with questions, asking, "What's wrong? Are you OK?"

I waved her off twice, saying "Nothing. It's nothing," but she kept prodding, hugging me tightly in the process. "Robin Williams committed suicide," I finally sputtered. I wept for about twenty seconds, then felt a mix of better and silly. Which is how I believe most people feel after crying in front of others.

Mommy was relieved, and more than a little amused by my answer. If anything, it made Mommy joyful.

"I can't say you don't have a soul anymore!" she cheered.

I'll remind her of that at the end of the next chick flick she drags me to, when she is sobbing and my eyes hurt from rolling.

I'm not positive what the point is in telling you all of this; I don't know what you're going to get out of it.

I think, in part, I wrote it because I don't know if I really know my father.

Yes, I know him, and we've had great father-son conversations… He's been wonderfully supportive of me, my life, my career…

And he loves you and Hillary.

But I'm not always sure I know just what makes him tick — what makes him think the way he does. Because of our dynamic, I'm not too bothered by that. But I don't want you to ever wonder about me.

I think I shared this with you in order to help you understand me better.

I hope that's not selfish.

Love,

Dad

August 20

Hey Buddy…

Your joy is in pushing things.

Your mini-lawnmower, toy trucks, small cars you have to bend all the way over in order to reach (in a way that would kill my back after three seconds but doesn't seem to bother you), and even Sister's baby doll stroller.

You grab hold and push, push, push.

Your favorite toy is a bumblebee on a stick from Grandpa Ned.

Grandpa Ned and Alice were visiting, and we were all at the Children's Museum. We had just walked in and you wandered off like you usually do. Nine times out of ten, you'll head over to the fish tanks. We find you saying hi to the turtle, and staring peacefully at the fish as they swim to and fro, hither and dither.

On this particular trip, however, you wandered into the gift shop.

Before anyone could stop you, you grabbed a bumblebee on a stick and began pushing it around gleefully. The toy had little balls on strings attached to the wheels; as they rolled, they clacked. You loved this. Loooooved this.

Mommy and I looked at one another with cautious eyes; taking the toy from you wasn't going to be fun. Fortunately, Grandpa Ned came to the rescue.

"I'll just buy it for him," he offered without prompting, and buy it he did. Generously and graciously, Grandpa Ned threw down his credit card, and the toy was yours.

You proceeded to push it around the Children's Museum for the entire trip.

It has been one year since that day, and you're still pushing it around joyfully.

The other day at daycare, I watched you through the door for a moment. You didn't see me, so you kept doing what you were doing: pushing a toy truck forever around a table. I watched you for at least two minutes, and all you did the entire time was walk around the table, incessantly pushing the truck.

It is almost your version of meditation. Pushing. Moving.

I cannot explain why it brings you such joy, just as I cannot explain why watching you push items about brings me such joy.

Sometimes, things are best left unexplained, and simply enjoyed.

Love,

Dad

August 27

Hey Buddy...

I am in Wausau, Wisconsin.

A few weeks ago, I wrote you a letter about rape. It was fairly harsh, but everything I wrote needed said.

Tonight, I'm feeling reflective.

I think there are two types of people you should take advice from: failures, and successes. The failure can tell you what he did wrong; the success can tell you what she did right.

If there's one thing I've accomplished, it's that I've both failed miserably at dating and succeeded beyond my wildest dreams at marriage. I've already written at length about relationships in my other scribblings, barfing up my failures in my first book and telling tales of marriage in the series of letters I wrote Sister. What I'm going to write about tonight is the gray area between dating and friendship.

In my past are two friends, Rachel and Felicity. They are from the same period of my life, don't know one another, and I didn't date either of them. I'm writing about them because while the initial arc of our relationships was similar, after a certain point in each relationship the paths diverge.

I was living in Los Angeles and coming out of a tumultuous relationship. As chance would have it, they were on the failing end of relationships as well. Having that in common, we first bonded over pain, and from there found commonalities that made us actual friends, not just folks sharing one similarity.

Rachel lived in Ohio; we met online. Felicity lived in Los Angeles, and we met through mutual friends. Eventually, each gave me an opening to make a move on them, and I remember both moments clearly.

In Rachel's case, I was on the road for comedy. She offered up her apartment as a crash pad between gigs, and when I arrived she insisted I sleep in her bed with her. When I balked at that offer, she started negotiating: "If you're uncomfortable getting in next to me, just sleep on the covers... We don't have to do anything."

I was having none of it. We had a very minor standoff which ended with me on the sofa like I wanted. In the morning we shared a nice breakfast, and I went on my merry way.

After that night, we remained great friends for years and years.

Switching to Felicity: she was at my place, and we were watching television while relaxing on my bed.

When the show ended, I asked, "What do you want to do now?"

She half-snuggled in next to me, making physical contact in a way that sent very clear signals, and asked, "Can't we just lay here? See what's on next?"

I got up, suggesting we should find something else to do. Go out to eat? Go on a hike? I don't remember exactly what, but anything involving leaving my apartment.

Felicity's mood turned on a dime. She was immediately outraged, and went from placid to furious. She started yelling, made it clear she just wanted to lie on the bed with me, and when she determined that wasn't going to happen, stormed off.

I didn't realize it at the time, but that was the end of our friendship; it was the last time I would ever see her. She stopped taking my calls and never returned any messages. Radio silence replaced the moments we used to get lunch or breakfast together, which was generally once or twice a week. After a couple of months, I stopped reaching out.

While I knew I had turned down her advances, I had no idea why she wouldn't let things go back to normal. Many of the friends I asked for advice regarding the situation—both male and female, mind you—believe that when Felicity made herself vulnerable that day on my bed and I rejected her, I insulted and hurt her deeply. I guess I agree with that line of thought, because there really is no other explanation. Putting yourself out there takes great courage; being spurned is embarrassing.

So, what was going through my mind in each of those cases? In a nutshell, I thought that both women were more emotionally invested in me than I was in them, and I didn't want to take advantage of that. In each case I didn't want to be either beholden and stuck in a relationship, or hurtful and just use either of them as a tool to achieve an orgasm.

Knowing Rachel better now than I did then, there's a strong chance I was wrong. But I'm OK with that, too. In some ways, and I could be completely off my rocker, I think that in the months and years after that night, Rachel came to appreciate my decision. She knew I wasn't rejecting her; I was respecting her as a friend.

Regarding Felicity... that's a bit trickier. I think the fact that we spent a lot of time together contributed to a mutual attraction. I liked Felicity, but I knew more about her relationship history than I wanted to. She tended to jump in deep and end up over her head quickly; that left me cautious.

We made really good platonic friends, and I just never got the sense I could be with her physically and not muck things up. There is no "best case" scenario when you become involved with someone who is more interested in you than you are them.

Why am I telling you all of this?

Because you're going to have to go through your own life and make choices regarding how to treat people. It comes down to the twin thoughts of: what can you sleep with at night? What can you live with looking back after the fact?

The best I can do is suggest you not take advantage of someone just because you can. I'm not limiting that statement to women and sex; I'm offering it up as a life guide. I'm suggesting you not take advantage of friendships, business relationships, or whatever else have you.

I don't want to suggest that it was my place to protect Rachel or Felicity. As grown women, they could each make their own decisions and didn't need me looking out for them. I just made the judgment call the best I could, and I stand by each.

Again, you'll have to make your own decisions in life; I cannot tell you what to do, I can only offer guideposts.

Love,

Dad

P.S. — I should point out that casual sex can be incredibly fun. By all means, have all the casual sex you want, just make sure both parties involved are on the same page. And wear a condom. Seriously. Wrap your wiener, Goddammit.

August 30

Hey Buddy...

You are two years and one month old. Early this morning, for the first time in your short life, you toddled out of your room and crawled into bed with your mother and me.

It happened at 1:20 a.m.

I know, because I was wide awake.

I had been awake for over an hour, just staring at the ceiling, with god-awful thoughts running through my head.

Earlier in the day, I clicked on a news story I had no right to read. In 2009, a seventeen-year-old girl named Brittanee went missing in South Carolina. On August 29, 2016, investigators finally uncovered her story.

Brittanee was abducted, gang-raped, held captive, beaten, shot, and fed to alligators.

Just writing that makes me want to throw up.

Before I was a father, I could read news stories like that and shake my head. I had no clue how people could be so indifferent to life, to others. I had no clue how people could be so cruel. But I could recover fairly easily.

Now that I'm a father, those stories haunt me.

And so, last night I was in bed, unable to sleep, horrific thoughts of worry and pain running through my mind. "What if something like that happened to Truman or Hillary?"

Once you start down such a horrible rabbit hole, there's no coming back. It just consumes you, and it absolutely consumed me.

All I want to do is protect you and Sister. To keep you happy, safe, fed, and warm.

Stories like that make me believe in fences and isolation; gated communities and home schooling. They're all illogical thoughts, yes, but fear will make you desperate.

So, there I was, awake in bed with evil thoughts in my head, when I heard your noise machine grow louder.

It meant you were up and opening your bedroom door.

You've never gotten up in the middle of the night before. Yes, it takes forever and a half to put you to bed, because you continually pop up and sneak out of your room... but when you do that, you always come out into the living room, or you go see what Sister is up to.

In the middle of the night, when you wake up you don't journey about the house. You cry.

I don't know what's going through your head—discombobulation, loneliness—but you cry. And then either Mommy or I—generally Mommy, because you prefer her to me by a wide margin—come in and soothe you, and you drift back to sleep.

Hearing your door open was different, because you hadn't cried first.

After a few moments, I heard our door open and I felt the dog move. He knew you were in the room and was lifting his head to check you out.

(You were, to be fair, not very stealthy. You entered carrying the Thomas the Train you fell asleep with, and were making a bit of a din.)

Next, you were at the foot of the bed, which was followed immediately by climbing up and crawling up to us. I remained still, and heard Mommy wake up.

"Hi sweetie," she greeted you as she moved a couple of pillows aside, creating space for you between us. "Lie down."

And lay down you did. But you were not comfortable. You squirmed and squirmed; Mommy reached over and held your hand, but it wasn't enough. You shuffled and squirmed, all the while kicking at me to move into a position more desirable to you. When you finally situated yourself you plopped your head right into the palm of my hand. It was as if my hand was a pillow; you immediately relaxed into me.

You stopped squirming, and a few moments later were making little snort noises.

You were asleep.

And like that, the evil thoughts about horrible people subsided.

They didn't vanish completely; they were still there. But instead of hammering at me, I was distracted by my love for you.

I'm not a person who puts much stock in the supernatural; I believe in logic more than anything. But I like the idea there's some sort of higher power out there, somewhere. It's why I'm agnostic and not a full-blown atheist. I can't say what that higher power might be—some people call it God—but there's a small part of me that believes there's... something.

I'd like to believe the reason you got out of bed last night instead of staying in there and crying when you woke up, is because...

...well, because I needed you.

I let you sleep for about five minutes in my hand, then gingerly slid it from underneath you so I could get comfortable and finally fall asleep myself.

Which I did. For probably ten minutes between 2 a.m. and 6 a.m.

I was trying so hard not to move and wake you up, that I disrupted my own slumber. Meanwhile, you weren't at all shy about taking whatever space you wanted in order to sleep, kicking me every time you needed to position yourself. At one point, you somehow managed to move to the foot of the bed and sleep alongside the dog.

It was hilarious, and—I can only imagine—the beginning of many, many nights of you sneaking into our bed when you wake in the middle of the night.

I'm looking forward to it.

Love,

Dad

September 2

Hey Buddy...

I am in Appleton, Wisconsin.

I lived here many years ago, and have the unfortunate memory of this city being my introduction into the world of racism. But let me go back a couple of years before my life in Appleton.

In October 1980, I was ten years old.

I lived in Milwaukee, Wisconsin, and attended the now-shuttered 38th Street School. At that time, the slide from middle-class neighborhood to decrepit ghetto had just begun.

I was a white face amid a sea of African-American students. I can recall a few Caucasian companions, but most of my friends had much darker skin than me. Which isn't to say I felt isolated, or different; as a child, what you are surrounded with is "normal." To me, having more black than white friends was what I knew, and was therefore hunky-dory.

There is one child whose name escapes me, but whose face I can bring up any time I choose. He was my age, and one morning we stood outside a classroom, talking.

Without warning, he whispered: "Mamma says if Reagan gets elected, black people gonna be back in the cotton fields."

I didn't really comprehend his words. As a ten-year-old, they held no historical context for me. But I understood his wide eyes, the nervousness in his voice, and his hesitant body language. My friend was afraid. The way his mother said those words instilled a chill in his bones, which he transferred to me.

My friend walked off, leaving me to digest the sentence.

Why would Reagan send black people to a cotton field?

Within a few years, my family would move twice, first to the aforementioned Appleton, and then Oconomowoc. The transition from big city urban to small city rural was informative; in each, I learned more about bigotry than I ever wanted to know. Slurs were tossed around casually, with the worst of the worst punctuating the air anytime black people were mentioned.

I was confused. I didn't know how to articulate my thoughts, but I knew that everyone in town was white, and they seemed to hate a race of people they never interacted with. I had no clue where the attitudes came from. I didn't know ignorance was handed down generation to generation. I didn't understand isolation, or the fear of interaction. I definitely wasn't familiar with media manipulation and how it feeds fear and stokes flames.

When confronted with racist attitudes, I remained silent. As a child, I wanted to fit in and be liked. I never joined the hatred jubilee; I just learned to bite my tongue.

That changed when I became a teenager, and hormones and anger overtook my shyness. I became more confident when confronting ignorance. Now, as an adult, I am probably more outspoken and belligerent than I should be.

On July 10, 2015, as you neared one year of age, South Carolina removed the Confederate flag from government buildings. As it tends to do, social media went crazy. The overwhelming consensus I saw was in support of the action. Unfortunately, even the most open-and-shut cases of integrity will have detractors.

On Facebook, one of my "friends" was a white girl in her twenties. She lived in Ohio, and was cute enough to have never had to self-examine or learn what white privilege is. Her post was a mix of vitriol and arrogance that ended with, "If you support the removal of the flag, then tell me so I can unfriend you!"

As a comedian, it's my job to expand my base of contacts. It helps me promote shows, sell merchandise, and grow my brand. But at what cost? This girl was a "fan," someone I was supposed to be courting. Instead of ignoring her post, I jotted down: "If supporting a symbol of racism is that important to you, feel free to delete me."

If I thought things would end there, I was wrong.

As many Facebook threads do, it quickly descended into chaos, anger, and horrible grammar. Ignorance is a glue that binds people. The like-minded find one another and cling together using "safety in numbers" as a shield against outside influence; they circle wagons, and latch arms. Soon many of her friends were flying the flag of the Confederate bandwagon.

All the usual terms were spewed forth: "Heritage!" "Freedom!" "Censorship!"

I responded with the standard facts: The Confederate flag is a symbol of racism, meant to signify the treasonous exit from the colonial United States. It was created solely for the idea of white supremacy.

Unfortunately, you cannot argue logic against passion, and passion can bring out the worst in people. Just when you think you've seen the nastiest slander possible, they surprise you with just how rotten they really are. I knew I was dealing with ugly, but even I was taken aback when I read the words: "Why can't they just get over it? They're not in the fields anymore!! Jews went through worse! Yet you don't hear Jewish people bring it up every single damn day they breath!"

(Breath being her word of choice, as opposed to the correct "breathe." Remember, I wasn't dealing with an intellectual here.)

I stared at the screen in furrowed-brow silence. Who would ever believe something so misguided, much less want to expose their spite to the world? How do you respond to such great levels of clueless? It is near impossible.

I could have explained that the "cotton fields" of 2015 were impoverished schools and gerrymandered voting districts that deny representation, or that "cotton fields" was a metaphor for a justice system that incarcerates African Americans at a disproportional rate than their white counterparts. Instead, I pointed out that Jewish people aren't witness to Nazi flags flying everywhere, especially on government buildings. While I didn't want to speak for anyone Jewish, I do believe if you were to ask one or two if they're "over" the Holocaust, I don't think the answer would be a cheerful thumbs up.

In my frustration, I also posted a popular meme insinuating those on the wrong side of the matter were stupid. To that, I was called a bevy of names.

So be it.

I don't know how to challenge willful ignorance without resorting to brutal shaming. I do not know how to teach those who ostrich their heads and act like children with fingers in their ears, shouting, "La-la-la-la I am not listening to Jeffrey but he is still talking!"

It is OK to defend beliefs. It is not OK to throw on blinders and ignore history.

True to her word, she unfriended me on Facebook, and I was a mix of happy and sad.

Happy, because someone like that is no longer even in the periphery of my life. To quote John McClane: "I got enough friends."

Sad, because it means the woman is entrenching herself further in a mix of unawareness and stupidity. Sad, because these people will vote against their own economic interests simply because they have misguided beliefs instilled in them from their parents and support circles. Sad, because it shows that racial progress is made in millimeters, not leaps and bounds.

A symbol of racism and treason shouldn't be debated or voted on; it should be removed, destroyed, and remembered in the history books as a dark period of our history we are supposed to have moved beyond.

It would be naïve to imagine racism will end during your lifetime; I am certain you will witness it just as I have. When I was younger, I used to think hatred would fade away by the time I was an adult. Surely we would be enlightened as a people in ten, twenty, or thirty years, right? Now, I look over the course of history and see that progress is so painfully slow that sometimes it feels like we're moving in reverse.

It will be on your shoulders to determine how you react to those mired in ignorance. Will you speak reason to them, or shout them down? I am too old a dog at this point to learn new tricks, but you... hopefully you will have more patience and better reasoning skills than I. Hopefully you will have the gift of gab, be able to pierce bubbles, and thus change minds and hearts. I will lay a foundation of acceptance and equality for you to build upon; what you do with it will be up to you.

The last time I drove past the 38th Street School, in maybe 2008 or 2009 and well before you were even an idea, the building was boarded up and the neighborhood looked like a war zone. It was a bleak area of economic ruin with little hope of a better life for any child living within its radius.

When I Googled my old stomping grounds before writing this note, the listing came up "Milwaukee College Preparatory School." Pictures online showed groomed grounds, and a remodeled building offering the hope of education to residents attempting to break free the chains of poverty.

Here's hoping every day is another millimeter away from those cotton fields.

Here's hoping you will live in a more tolerant time than I did.

Love,

Dad

September 10

Hey Buddy...

I am in Minneapo... wait, no. I'm technically in St. Paul, Minnesota. With the Twin Cities, it's best to keep track of where you are and not insult one by claiming it is the other.

Anyway, I read an article earlier titled, "Why I'll Never Date a Feminist."

It went slightly viral, which is how I discovered the piece. Someone shared it online, then someone else commented on it... that's how things get out there.

With this piece, the title alone made all the right people outraged. So much so, I have to wonder if the author of the piece wasn't just trolling for fun.

After reading it, I thought about writing an empathetic, thoughtful response about why I married a feminist. I imagined writing about your mother, and Sister. I imagined talking about how I believed in equality for them, and how I occasionally feared for their safety. I considered discussing my belief in Title IX, and my disgust at the pay disparity between women and men.

But the more I tried to write that, the less I liked it. The less I liked even the idea of it.

The reality of the situation is: I didn't marry a feminist because I believe in Title IX, or because I respect women, or because I believe in equal pay, or — when the time comes — because I want Sister to be safe on her college campus.

No.

I believe in those things because it's the right thing to do. Those beliefs are gimmies. "Duh" beliefs.

("Do I want my daughter to be safe? Duh. Do I think men and women should be paid equally? Duh.")

So the short answer, then, is that I married a feminist because I fell in love with one.

I fell in love with a strong, intelligent woman. One I hope helps me raise strong, intelligent children.

Add to that — and here's the important part — I'm comfortable enough in my own skin to be married to a strong, intelligent woman.

After we got engaged, Mommy approached me with something she thought might be a problem: she wanted to keep her own name. She didn't want my surname, and she didn't want to hyphenate. She liked the name she was given at birth.

I shrugged. There wasn't even a discussion.

I didn't puff out my chest or put forth any idiotic reasons about it being an attack on my masculinity, against "tradition," or any other nonsense. Mommy's name made her happy, marrying me made her happy, and those two things seemed perfectly reasonable, independent things.

That's why people refer to Mommy as "Lydia Fine," and me as "Nathan Timmel."

(I'm sure that when you and Sister become teenagers, you will use this against us. When angry with Mommy, you'll bellow "I'm glad I don't have your name," and when upset with me you'll shout "I want to change my last name!" It's something I'm looking forward to. Not.)

When you look at men's rights activists, or online trolls attacking women, or the author of "Why I'll Never Date a Feminist," you're generally dealing with insecure...

I almost wrote "men" there, but they don't deserve that label. Let me start again.

The truth is, when you look at men's rights activists, or online trolls attacking women, or the author of "Why I'll Never Date a Feminist," you're generally dealing with insecure boys. These are people who feel threatened by the world around them, so they lash out at it in a feeble attempt to look tough — to project "macho."

The author of the "I'll Never Date" piece is an overweight, balding, blemish-faced buffoon. He looks like a young Karl Rove, and no matter what your political leanings are, everyone can agree Karl Rove is not an attractive man.

(Yes, I know you will have to Google that reference. It is what it is.)

I do not believe for one second the author of the "I'll Never Date" piece has his pick of the litter when it comes to dating, and I tell you this: any man getting laid on the regular isn't worried about feminists destroying their way of life. They're too busy dating, enjoying sex with, and marrying women to belittle or degrade them.

Reactionaries who are angry at the world around them? They're the lot passive-aggressively condemning the women who won't go out with them. Instead of working on personal growth or change, they point fingers and lay blame. It's sad, but easy.

(And people love easy.)

Unlike many, I wasn't angry when I read the "I'll Never Date" piece. In fact, I wish more men would advertise their failings so blatantly. It's much easier to know up front who you don't want to interact with than to find out somewhere down the road they're racist, sexist, homophobic, or the like.

I've said this repeatedly in my letters to you, but it's always worth repeating: you will learn how to treat women through watching me interact with your mother. Every behavior in life is learned; everything starts at home.

You might have friends who are louts, and you might be tempted to try and fit in with them, but it will be my duty as your father to get you through such times. Not through force or intimidation, but a clear sense of self, and knowledge of right and wrong.

Wish me luck.

Love,

Dad

September 16

Hey Buddy…

Tonight I am in Sioux Falls, South Dakota. The show was… not fun. And that's putting it mildly.

I've been doing this a long time, and learned long ago that comedy is not always about artistic expression; sometimes you're just earning a mortgage payment. That's what tonight was, a gig to pay the bills. And man, I earned my money.

It was a corporate event—a private party for a flooring firm. Everyone was tired, and somewhat bitter.

Before taking the stage, I was told, "There are kids here," which is just about death to a comedy show. I asked what having kids in the audience meant to them, and further asked what they wanted out of me. I explained that while I can do a clean, PG-rated show, I would struggle to perform for "all ages."

(Technically, they should have told me about the kids before ever hiring me, so I could turn the gig down, which I do when I feel I'm in over my head.)

My contact, Amy, said, "They know it's an adult comedy show, but they brought kids anyway. That's on them, but please keep it as clean as possible."

I asked if innuendo was OK, and was given the thumbs up.

No swearing, no politics, nothing divisive, but I could play with themes. I can do that.

Then I found out they would be giving away prizes after my set, the highlight of which was a trip to Hawaii. The course of the evening was to be:

- Cocktails
- Dinner
- Comedy
- Door prizes

I winced. This is never the way you want to run an event. By putting door prizes at the end, you're forcing people who want to go home to stick around and see if they've won the TV or $100 or trip to Hawaii.

But, it's not my place to tell anyone how to run their event; I was just there to do as I'm told.

Which I did, and... ouch.

From the moment I was introduced, they stared at me. I got a smattering of polite introductory applause, but that was it. After that, the room was divided. About 15 percent laughed and had a good time. Maybe 55 percent smiled. But that final 30 percent? They stared. And frowned. And crossed their arms. And 30 percent of a room gone silent kills all the energy.

I did jokes that usually got applause breaks, and these people chuckled at best. Most jokes that got good laughs everywhere else got the occasional smile. At one point, I did a joke that has never failed to receive applause, and it got silence. I was so stunned I even said, "Wow. That's the first time that joke hasn't worked."

I plowed forward, did my contracted time, and got off stage shaken.

I talked to two of the women in charge — Amy and a nice woman named Sarah — and they told me, "Everyone was just so tired. We've been putting in 10-hour days all week and people just want to go home. We should have had this on Saturday, given people a day to rest. This is how it is every year. They never give it up for the comedian."

Though inside my head I screamed, then why do you keep having comedians?!, I smiled and nodded in silence.

As I said, this one wasn't for me, this one was for the money.

A cruel truth to my business.

But, it paid well, and tomorrow I will be back home to you, Mommy, and Sister. I don't know what we'll do with our Saturday, but it will be nice being home for two full days of the weekend, instead of one.

Love,

Dad

September 23

Hey Buddy...

I am in La Crosse, Wisconsin tonight. I'm smiling as I write, because many hours ago you received a great surprise: Graw Janet and Bada Joe picked you and Sister up from daycare.

The last time Graw Diane visited us, she arrived while you and Sister were still at daycare. When it came time to pick you up, she came with me. When she entered your room? Wow. Your eyes went wide and you pointed, exclaiming to everyone within earshot, "That's my gamma!!"

Your teachers all laughed warmly as you rushed to her for hugs.

Which means I'm smiling at the moment, because I can only assume you were doubly delighted today to see two grandparents come wandering into your classroom.

I'll be home tomorrow; it's another two-day weekend under my own roof for me. It's nice—I have this paying gig tonight, and Saturday I hold my seventh-annual Comedy for Charity show.

As you grow, learning to give is going to be an important part of your life.

When we go to the grocery store, we always buy one extra item. Just one. At home, we put that item into a special bag. When that bag is full we take it to the local food pantry.

It's not much, admittedly, but it's what we can afford, and every little bit helps. Our one box of cereal helps one family. Our extra bag of pasta can give dinner to children in need.

Food aside, every year I put together a comedy show for charity. A local bar donates its space, comedians donate their time, and we try and do a little good for the world. In the past six years I've raised $18,000 and given it all away.

The money has gone to Iowa veterans returning home from war, private families in need because of medical emergencies, firefighters, and pediatric cancer research. This year we're collecting winter clothes and cash.

I started the show on a whim.

A woman in Mommy's office was going through a hard time. Her husband had been in a car accident, and was in a coma. Though insurance was covering most costs, the bills were piling up and they needed help.

I asked if my putting together a show and giving them the money would help, and holy poop on a stick, it did help. The venue sold out, and we raised thousands of dollars.

After that, I was hooked.

Performing comedy, and giving the money to good causes? Count me in. There have been some great audiences in the past, and my fingers are crossed for tomorrow.

Writing the words "great audiences" reminded me of last weekend — my not-so-great audience.

It hasn't been a good week, Buddy.

In my last note to you, I wrote of a flooring company that hired me to perform at their private party. It wasn't a fun show, to say the least. I got up, did my thing, and they just stared at me.

There are times when a performer is bad, and there are times when the audience is bad. This was absolutely a case of the audience not wanting to laugh.

If you remember, Amy, the woman in charge told me, "This is how it is every year. They never give it up for the comedian."

Yeah, well, despite her reassurance to me, she emailed the booking agent and complained about me. She said I did a bad job, which makes me exceedingly angry.

The booking agent then sent me a terse email on Tuesday; contained within was the email Amy had sent him. It contained the sentence, "I told Nathan there were kids there!"

She neglected to tell the booking agent what she told me: "The parents of those kids know it's an adult show."

Which shouldn't matter, because I still performed a clean show. I didn't swear, I didn't bring up politics, I didn't discuss anything overly sexual or remotely controversial. I got on stage and from moment one they weren't there for me.

Even worse, my liaison, Amy, said she received the complaint: "I had to sit through that 'comedian' in order to see if I won a door prize."

Somehow, that was my fault. I knew putting entertainment before the giveaway was a horrible idea, but there was nothing I could do about it.

Anyway, the booking agent is mad at me, and as of right now I don't know if he'll ever give me work again.

Which is part of the reason my job can be so soul-crushing at times.

I went into a hostile environment, was both professional and funny, the client and the audience were awful, and somehow that's my fault. And there's nothing I can do about it.

I don't want this letter to be defeating or negative; it's just... a life lesson for you, I suppose.

Sometimes you can do everything right, and it won't matter. You will be blamed for things you didn't do. You will be innocent, yet guilty.

It doesn't happen often, but when it does, it's frustrating, and painful. All you can do is pick yourself up, brush yourself off, and move on.

Even worse, I reached out to the booking agent after his initial harsh email to me. As politely as possible—and I even had Mommy vet the letter for me to make sure I wasn't being snide or passive aggressive—I explained that I have been doing my job for many years, and given the fact I have two very young children at home, there was no way I was going to enter a situation and harm my earning potential. Because if I did, how would I feed my kids? I asked how I received all the positive testimonials on my webpage if my modus operandi was to be inappropriate or unprofessional.

I received no response. The booking agent was as silent as the audience that night, and there's not a thing I can do about it.

Not a thing, except brush it off, square my shoulders, and keep moving forward.

Love,

Dad

P.S. — An update: I'm reviewing this letter with over a month's perspective. The booking agent still refuses to hear me out, but the charity show was a success. Standing room only, with about $2,000 worth of winter gear and cash raised. That's $20,000 in seven years. I'm proud of that. I still struggle with anger toward the booking agent, but I'm proud of what I've been able to do for the community.

October 12

Hey Buddy...

What makes you so sad sometimes?

The neat thing about having two kiddos is discovering your disparate personalities. Sister always wakes up sluggish. You wake up in one of two moods: ready to go, or devastated. OK, sometimes you wake up giggling, but usually it's raring to go, with the occasional crying. When you wake in tears, I always wonder what's wrong.

Today at daycare, I held you for over ten minutes. You clung to me as I attempted to drop you off; I sat on the floor and hugged you as you cried (and snotted) into my shoulder. There was no real reason for it, or at least nothing I could discern.

Everything started at home. You cried when you woke up, cried as you half-ate your cereal, and you cried the entire way to school, alternately demanding "Roxanne!" and, after I would queue up "Roxanne," crying harder and yelling "No Roxanne! No Roxanne!"

Naturally, when I paused the song, you would resume shouting "Roxanne!" again.

All this excess emotion made it difficult to figure out what you wanted.

You usually rush to your classroom immediately; when we walk into daycare, you're off and running. Sometimes I haven't even completed checking you in when I hear "Hi Truman!" from afar; you've already made it to your room.

Not today.

Today there were so many tears. Days like these are random, but when they arrive you're inconsolable.

I held you, and quietly sang "Roxanne" into your ear until you calmed somewhat, and then Miss Nicole took my place. You started sobbing again, but calmed when offered your morning snack.

"Roxanne," by the way, is what I sing to you at bedtime. Several weeks ago, and I'm not sure why, Mommy started singing to you at bedtime. She snuggles with you and takes requests. You giggle and ask for "Roll Call" from Thomas & Friends—which you delightfully call "Thomas and the Train" for some reason—or the theme to Super Why.

Unfortunately, I don't know the lyrics to those songs. When it's my turn to get you into bed, I channel my inner Sting and offer poor renditions of "Roxanne" and "Every Little Thing She Does is Magic."

(Which, like Sister—because you learned to do so from her—you call "Eee-oh." As speech isn't quite your thing yet, you cannot say "every little thing she does is magic." You can, however, say "Want eee-oh!" and I know exactly what mean.)

I'm sorry I'm not much for traditional bedtime songs, but I'm glad you enjoy what I have to offer.

You've been sleeping through the night somewhat better, by the way, but you still wake up randomly, crying, in the middle of the night. Not every night, but more often than not. Maybe every

228

other night or every third night you make it through without waking.

When I try and go in to console you, it just doesn't work. In those moments, you want Mommy, and Mommy alone. Mommy's touch soothes your sorrow.

I worry that you inherited Mommy's night terrors. She's had them for years, since well before I met her.

Every so often she'll wake and say something odd, or reach out and grab me. In her mind, I am falling out of bed and she's catching me. In reality, I'm just lying there, asleep, being awoken by a firm grip.

Mommy falls back asleep quickly, but you not so much. I wonder what is going through your mind in those moments — what has you waking and crying.

I hope it fades, but if not, we'll explain to you what night terrors are, and you'll do fine growing up with them. Just a little something to deal with is all.

You're still our perfect little boy, and we love you.

Even if you don't let us sleep.

Love,

Dad

October 17

Hey Buddy…

Well, for the first time in over four years, Mommy and I went away somewhere… alone.

Shocking, I know.

Yes, I travel for work often, and every once in a while you are left to my devices while Mommy is out and about, but for the first time since becoming parents, Mommy and I left you and Sister home for more than just a date night.

We went to Los Angeles, California, leaving you in the care of Graw Diane, and it is a lengthy tale…

Years and years ago, I lived in Los Angeles. Upon moving there, I met a comedian named Mike. He was a nice and funny fellow, and told me a story about his first experience with Hollywood.

"I got cast in a movie," he began, naming a big-budget sports comedy I had seen and enjoyed. "I was the 'bad guy,' so to speak. Every time the hero's team played mine, he and I would get into it. I told everyone. My friends, family, strangers… it was my big break. Then the movie came out and I had been cut from every scene. It was so embarrassing."

His story always stuck with me as a cautionary tale against touting your achievements too quickly. Which leads me to why Mommy and I were in California.

It began with an email.

"Hi Nathan, I'm an associate producer for a syndicated talk show based in Los Angeles. I read an article you wrote about how your wife makes more money than you, and we're doing an episode on breadwinning wives next week. I wondered if you two would be interested in coming on and discussing your experience."

I was a mix of ambivalent and game, so I forwarded it to my better half. She was curious, and said I should shoot the producer a reply. From there, a back-and-forth began — emails, followed by phone calls. We went up the power chain from associate producer to producer, each time answering more and more questions. What were we like as people? What was our story? How was our marriage? How did we respond to questioning?

In reality, they were only asking one thing: would we make good guests?

After a final, thirty-minute speakerphone conversation with the two of us, it was decided yes. We were just what they were looking for, and things began moving forward in earnest.

But there was a problem: they wanted us there Thursday, to film on Friday. Mommy had an engagement on Thursday night — a concert in Minneapolis, which is four hours from our home. There were no red eye flights; would it be possible to leave crack-of-dawn Friday and fly in the day of the show?

The producer was concerned, and decided that wasn't possible.

If anything happened — a flight delay, day-of-show traffic — the entire schedule would be thrown off. We had to arrive in California on Thursday, or we weren't viable guests.

Mommy was torn. Being on TV might be fun, but was it worth cancelling her plans; worth skipping a concert she had waited months for (and spent a lot of money on)? Channeling her inner Vulcan, Mommy determined that logically she could attend a different performance. TV shows, however, didn't come a-knocking every day. She offered her tickets to Aunt Jessica as a BOGO, eating the cost of one in the process.

Crunch time began. We had to film and edit an introductory video to send in. I had to make a B-roll video of me performing at various comedy clubs. We had to comb through pictures and fire off as many as we could for the talk show to pick and choose from. We had to contact photographers and obtain releases, and we had to sign 1,000 forms (and fill out a few others) ourselves. Mommy requested two vacation days from work; Graw Diane agreed to take care of you and Sister.

With all ducks in a row, we were off; Hollywood awaited. Our bags were packed with the several outfit options wardrobe had requested as we flew into LAX, got shuttled to our hotel, and went to bed exhausted.

The next day started out fine.

We and the other two guests were picked up at the hotel and taken to the studio. Along the way, we got to know one another. As the theme was "Breadwinning Wives," it turned out Mommy and I were The Couple That Made it Work. Next was a woman whose marriage had fallen apart because she out earned her husband, and the final guest was a consultant who helped companies make their workplace better for female breadwinner employees. It all made sense.

At the studio, we went into hair and makeup and were given a final meeting with the producer. The rundown was: we would be seated in a special area between the audience and the stage. In segments one and two, the host would interview his special guest, a contestant from an old show called The Celebrity Apprentice. Segment three was Mommy and me, four the divorcee, five the consultant, and six a panel of the three female guests.

Good times.

We were escorted into the studio-proper where I noticed something odd; the audience didn't match the show's demographic. Just as you wouldn't expect to see sixty-year-old lumberjacks in the studio audience of The View, what I saw in the stands didn't make sense with this show.

I didn't have time to dwell on it, though, as we were seated and told everything was about to begin. The host arrived, announced the contestant-guest, and we were off to the races. The contestant was a high-energy snake oil saleswoman. Everything was dramatic, loud, and unfortunately lacking substance.

"You need to be financially independent!" she shouted. "Start your own eBay store today! Clean out your closet! Sell your junk! Get paid!"

I plastered a robotic smile across my face and applauded politely, but inside was thinking, "How would an online yard sale make you financially independent? How do you restock your inventory: buy new and sell used?"

I also wondered what the contestant had to do with breadwinning wives.

The first segment ended; the second began. More gestures and more overjoyed shouting about starting eBay stores occurred.

Then something awkward happened.

We had been told the host would ask us a question during segment two. What they didn't tell us was that the question would be somewhat loaded.

One thing Mommy and I made clear throughout our conversations with the producers was: this situation works for us. My male ego isn't disrupted by the fact she out earns me, and she doesn't feel we've sacrificed anything as a family due to our dynamic.

So when she was asked, "What have you sacrificed?" Mommy was thrown.

She answered the best she could, and then the host asked how I felt. I gave the answer I had given during every pre-interview: "I'm fine with it. My wife is awesome, and it doesn't sting a bit that she's the breadwinner."

Then the contestant-guest jumped in and told me to start my own online store.

I smiled mechanically and tried to hide an eye roll.

The second segment ended… and the contestant-guest remained in place. Mommy and I looked at one another.

"I think we just got bumped," I whispered.

Just then she saw the word "NO" followed by her name being typed on to the teleprompter.

While still on break, the contestant-guest shouted over to us, "Do you feel better about your situation now? Did my advice help?"

Mommy and I were confused. Our situation? We didn't have a situation; we were good.

I sort of shrugged and played dumb. Mommy answered hesitantly: "We... actually already have viable side projects. Both of us." I could tell she wanted to be honest — start an eBay store? Are you insane? — but wasn't sure if she should be.

The contestant-guest smiled and gave us a thumbs up before turning back to her handlers.

The third segment started, and we weren't introduced. When the section ended with the host saying, "Next up, a divorcee..." we knew we had been cut.

The consultant went up after the divorcee, and while Mommy was invited to be a part of the final panel segment, everything seemed pointless by then.

The show wrapped up, and we were escorted back to our dressing room. The producer came in and said things had "gotten away from them." She wasn't contrite.

In the end, it was a wash. For the most part, we laughed. Mommy and I couldn't believe they flew us all the way across the country for nothing. At the same time, given the hassle of everything — from the insane amount of phone interviews and forms, to arranging child care — as well as the fact Mommy could have gone to her concert? Well, that was frustrating.

While waiting for the shuttle to the hotel, Mommy decided, "The only part I didn't like was feeling expendable. If someone had come over during the break and told us, 'We're so sorry, we're going to have to cut your segment,' it would have been fine." The fact we had to figure out in real time we were being shoved aside bothered her. Which I get, but that's how Hollywood works.

Hollywood doesn't apologize. It does what it wants and moves on.

Still, it's all good, and in fact the funniest moment came as we were preparing to leave. With a happy smile upon her face, the producer told us: "We'll tell you when your episode airs!"

I whispered to Mommy, "Why? So we can watch ourselves not be on TV? We do that every day."

She laughed.

It was still a neat experience. To be thought of in the first place, to be flown to L.A., put up in a hotel... it was a free mini-vacation, and you can't complain about that.

When it all began, I suggested we not tell anyone until everything was over. I had learned well from my friend Mike and knew it would be better to be cautious rather than plaster our social media accounts with "We're gonna be on TV!!!"

Turns out, that was a good move.

I will say this, however: When the divorcee went up for her segment, a member of the audience came down to fill her seat. I leaned over to the eager fellow and whispered, "Central Casting?"

"Yes!" he enthused. "This is my third time here."

I smiled. Of course they were using Central Casting. The live audience was made up of paid actors and actresses in waiting — people looking for any toe-in-the-door they could find into the industry. That's why they looked so out of place.

(Before we left, I discussed this with a production assistant. He confirmed that most of the audience was indeed paid to be there.)

One final thought: when the contestant-guest asked if we felt better about our situation, I believe the question was genuine. I don't know what information she was given, and conflict does make for better television than "Everything is A-OK." Maybe we were presented as a couple in trouble. Maybe she thought our marriage was fraught with tension. She probably thought we needed help, and it was kind of her to offer it. Still, I won't be starting an eBay store anytime soon.

But if any other talk shows want to fly us somewhere, put us up in a nice hotel and not use us?

We're in. And maybe next time you and Sister will be old enough to come with us.

Love,

Dad

October 24

Hey Buddy…

Oh, the differences between boys and girls.

Today we went to a new park in our hometown.

It's Monday, which means it's Daddy Daycare Day.

Because of my travel schedule, you and Sister have to be in daycare at least part time. Daycare is a hot commodity here, because in less than ten years our small city has grown by over 8,000 people.

We live in a "bedroom community," meaning people either commute twenty minutes north or fifteen minutes south in order to work. They return to sleep and raise their families.

Point being: we cannot pick and choose daycare hours as they relate to my work schedule. We can't pay for daycare when I'm gone, then keep it on standby when I'm home. Daycare wants paying customers, and though we don't need it every week, we need it often enough.

Plus, it's good for you and Sister to socialize, and the teachers there are more focused than I could ever be; you and Sister actually learn days, numbers, and letters at daycare. At home you learn very little.

(Daddy is a bit of a slacker. Sorry.)

Also — and this took a while for Mommy to realize — it helps you learn what life will be like as you deal with a revolving door of different teachers over the course of your life. Sister recently got a teacher that wasn't her favorite. Mommy even worried a little bit about the tone of voice the teacher used, but I liked it. While most everyone in the daycare is as gentle as a kitten, the new teacher had a little bark to her.

This made Sister hesitant when entering her room, which is good. Best to learn early in life that you're not going to love every person you come in contact with. Best to learn early on that life is full of a wide variety of people. Some you will enjoy, others not as much. Sometimes, though, you have to learn how to interact with them; life isn't about isolation and only being around people you choose to be around.

Yes, you will be friends and lovers with people you gel with, but you need to learn how to be around every sort of person imaginable, even those you disagree with or not even like. It's good for your personal growth.

Anyway, getting back to the point of this nonsense, we are allowed to keep you in daycare part time, saving us a few bucks. Every Monday you and Sister are both with me, and today we went to our city's newest park. Which, as chance would have it, was built right across from what is probably our city's oldest park.

The new park has modern structures — climbable fun for toddlers, pristine swings, and even a zip line. The old park has rusted swings, and across a bite-sized creek — something barely containing water and easily traversed by even your wobbly, two-year-old uncertain legs — a slide.

A very twisty, spiral, metal slide.

You both wanted to go down it, and who am I to stop you?

(Oh, right, your father. Well, see above where I admit to being a slacker.)

As you and Sister are a little too young to have full control of your bodies, when you each went down the spiral slide, you lost your center of gravity and spun too hard, eventually bonking your head against the slide's hard, metal side wall.

Sister exited while rubbing her head in irritation, and went off to play in the sandbox. Fool me once.

You, on the other hand, made me laugh and laugh and laugh. You went down the slide, twisting and bonking your head, and climbed off the bottom rubbing your noggin just like Sister.

You even looked right at me and said—a mix of anger and sadness in your voice—"Ow! Bonk head!"

And then you headed right back to the stairs, climbing up them to go down the slide again. Live and don't learn, apparently.

Every time you slid down I'd hear the hard metallic thud! sounding as you hit the third twist.

And every time you exited the slide you rubbed your head in pain, yelling "Ow! Bonk head!" at me.

And then it was straight back to the stairs for another round. It was so funny and adorable and stereotypical of young boys: When something hurts, do it again because it was fun.

You repeated this action five times before getting your fill; I wondered if I was going to have to initiate concussion protocol.

Eventually we meandered back to the new, safer park, and you and Sister enjoyed climbing what there is to climb, sliding down the plastic slide, and zip lining repeatedly.

Most people dislike Mondays.

I love my Mondays.

Love,

Dad

October 29

Hey Buddy...

I am in Brighton, Michigan.

On the plus side of this weekend, I got to stay with some good friends of mine, Matt and Chuck. On the negative side of this weekend, the World Series decimated anyone's interest in live entertainment. The Friday show was cancelled, and tonight's show had six people at it. Six! Wooooo!

Anyway, I've been friends with Matt and Chuck for years. Matt is an artist—a painter, specifically. We have several works by him in our house. For the first year of your life, one hung in your room. Mommy framed it in glass, and the painting was of a heart, and padlock.

The painting was a holdover from when the room was Sister's. It always hung above the crib, and when she switched rooms, we left it up. Mommy and I figured it was more a nursery painting than something connected to Sister herself.

We never thought anything of having it over your crib, because Sister wasn't a kicker. When we put her to bed, she went to bed. You, on the other hand, were a crib kicker. Now that you're in a toddler bed, you're a wanderer. But when you were confined by high railings you couldn't climb? Your only amusement was to kick-kick-kick to your heart's delight.

One night, you kicked the painting right off the wall. You were pounding away on your crib below it, and the vibrations were strong enough to knock it from its moorings. Fortunately, the painting slid straight down, dropping between the crib and the wall to the floor. Mommy and I heard the thud from the living room and came in quickly to investigate.

When we saw what had happened, we breathed a sigh of panicked relief. We looked at one another with fearful eyes, imagining what could have happened. Instead of the painting sliding straight down and landing on the floor, it could have clipped the edge of the crib, fallen forward, and landed on you. Mommy and I both shuddered, thoughts of the glass breaking, and shards flying into your eyes.

When Sister was born, we went through the house filling sockets with plugs and strapping furniture to the walls. But a sheet of glass hanging above your crib? Somehow that escaped our investigations. The guilt Mommy and I would have carried to our graves had something happened to you that day is unimaginable.

With a shudder at that memory, I return to Matt and Chuck.

They are married, which means (if you haven't figured it out), they are gay. I only bring that up because the three of us talked a little about advancements the LGBTQ community has made recently. Unfortunately, we had to admit progress is incremental.

For some reason, even in 2016 there is still bigotry toward homosexuals. Less so than when I was growing up, but enough to still be mind boggling. It seems as if no amount of progress matters to some people; they just hate, and nothing pierces their belief system.

I'm not sure exactly how you change minds and hearts, but I have an idea. It involves emotion, not reason, and in some ways that makes me sad. I think we should make decisions based on realities, not feelings, but that doesn't seem to work all that often.

My reasoning goes all the way back to high school. Tenth grade, to be specific. That's when I took speech class. Students were being taught to overcome one of life's biggest fears: public speaking.

Throughout the course of a semester, we had to prepare and perform a series of standard lectures. Styles included (but were not limited to) informative, narrative, and persuasive. I have no clue how I landed on the topic of my persuasive speech — euthanasia — but I do know that I chose it myself. Topics were not assigned by the teacher.

I was unfamiliar with euthanasia. Hell, in 10th grade I was entirely ignorant of the word, much less its meaning. But the more I read, the more intriguing I found the subject. The idea people could be in control of their own medical decisions, especially one that would end their life? Fascinating.

I stood before the class and delivered a matter-of-fact talk. Allowing people with debilitating diseases to exit their life with grace and dignity made euthanasia a "this just makes sense" idea. If my words contained any empathy, it was generated, like an actor might emote for a scene. It wasn't a heartfelt speech by any measure. I was catering to reason, and pleading with people to do what was right for the sake of being right.

Whether or not my speech was any good or changed any minds, I do not remember; at the forefront of my mind is what happened at the end of the year. For the final speech, students could choose from the variety of styles learned over the semester. A boy in my class, Mike, chose persuasion. His topic? Euthanasia. Mike wanted to go head-to-head with my pro stance with a hard con; Mike was 100% against the practice.

Where I had spoken emotionlessly of the benefits of euthanasia, Mike stood in front of the class and cried. He broke down and openly wept as he said the words, "I don't want anyone to kill my grandpa."

Numerous students welled up, and after all was said and done Mike received many, many hugs. Meanwhile, I sat in the back of the class with a furrowed brow.

Mike hadn't actually challenged anything I said; he didn't discuss personal rights, the opportunity to exit life with a sense of dignity versus weathered and incapacitated in a hospital bed, or gone into patient's decisions or medical costs. Mike ignored everything but emotion. It was a killer move.

Whether or not his grandfather was suffering or wanted to escape whatever was ailing him — cancer, Parkinson's, what have you — was immaterial. Mike didn't want anyone to "kill his grandpa." Mike took the idea people could make their own health decisions and turned it into something an uneducated politician would later call "Death Panels."

In his mind, Mike's grandpa wasn't deciding to end his own suffering; someone was killing him.

That's when I learned that people are, at their base, emotional creatures. You can give them facts, proof, and solid intellectual arguments, but in the end they will follow their heart or gut. People respond to emotion more than dispassionate intellect.

Sadly, even though I know this, I'm still not adept at using emotion to get my own points across. To this day I still beat my head against the intellectual wall, forever frustrated by the truth "this is factually sound" doesn't always matter to people. Maybe I see using emotion as a weapon as manipulation. Maybe that makes me a cold person. I don't know. I know I'm not always good at reaching people, but I'm forever attempting to improve.

So what's the point of all of this?

I can't tell you how to interact with people you disagree with; I can only tell you where I've gone wrong. Whenever I stumble across someone who is racist, sexist, or homophobic, I do my best to reason with them. When that fails, I turn to mockery. I know this is inappropriate, and yet I succumb to my own shortcomings time and time again.

I don't know what issues will divide us as a people as you grow, but I suspect it will be the same old same old: race, sexuality, gender, and religion. Those subjects have forever kept us separate. It is unfortunate.

You will have to respond to people who are limited in thought as you best see fit. You can reason with them, or you can try and reach them on an emotional level.

I wish I was better at the latter.

Love,

Dad

November 5

Hey Buddy...

I take you and Sister to the library every Monday.

We return our stack of books from the previous week, and then Sister runs around grabbing new tomes for me to soothe the two of you to sleep with. She tends to choose books according to what's on the cover, which means that when we check out I carry a stack of princesses, baby animals, and other such items that tend to appeal to young girls.

(You, for the record, head straight to the computers. There are several learning games on them that enthrall you.)

On Monday, Sister threw a book titled *I Am Jazz* into the pile.

In keeping with every other item, the cover contained an illustration of a little girl pretending to be a mermaid. "That's why she grabbed this" crossed my mind, but beyond that I didn't give it another thought. I didn't examine the back, read the jacket, or delve any deeper into what the book was about.

That night, as always, Sister chose three books to read before bed. *I Am Jazz* was first on the list.

"This is number one, Daddy," she told me with her serious face.

It is very important I read her books in the correct order. If I were to read book number two before book number one? Well, that would cause crying, and mass hysteria. Dogs and cats living together. That sort of thing. Mostly crying.

I found *I Am Jazz* somewhat bland at first. The first few pages were filled with little simplicities—"I like princess gowns, I like cartwheels..."—and so on and so forth.

Then I turned a page.

I read the words aloud before fully realizing what they said. And then I paused. And then a wide smile spread across my face and I started laughing. What I discovered was a bigger twist than M. Night Shyamalan has ever created, and it was absolutely more brilliant than his nonsense.

"I have a girl brain but a boy body. This is called transgender."

After I recovered from my giggle-fit of surprise, I continued reading. From that page forward was a delightfully modest and straightforward explanation of what it means to be transgender. The child in question, Jazz herself, was treated with dignity, respect, and above all else, normalcy.

"I have a girl brain but a boy body." That's it in a nutshell. Some people are born different, and different is OK.

The book touched on bullying and visiting a doctor for the official diagnosis, but as a children's book it didn't go too far into these subjects. It's not supposed to; it is a perfect introduction to a marginalized population finally being normalized by society, if only in the tiniest of baby steps.

Sister enjoyed the tale, and even though she doesn't realize it yet, she's learning an important lesson about life. The book is a wonderful presentation of "different from me, but the same as me."

The next night, I read *I Am Jazz* to both of you.

You didn't appreciate it as much as, say, Thomas & Friends, but you'll get it someday. Even though it's over your head at the moment, with lessons like those contained in *I Am Jazz*, it's best to start early. If someone is instilled with love and acceptance from the beginning of their life, then bigotry will find no home in their head or heart.

I'm writing this on a Saturday afternoon, meaning it's been several days since our trip to the library. In the interim, I've read the book to the two of you nightly, and have come across Sister leafing through it randomly throughout the week. She'll be in her chair or on her bed, whispering to herself happily: "I like cartwheels."

While cartwheels might not be the point of the book, what's important is that when Sister heard, "I have a girl brain but a boy body," she didn't flinch. She accepted it as normal, which it is. Some people are born in the wrong body for their gender, and sometimes they are able to transition into the correct body. That's — as Old Blue Eyes sang — life.

When you start to comprehend what the book is about, I don't think you'll flinch, either. You might ask questions, but that's normal. America is still coming to terms with what it means to be LGBTQ, but the more children that grow up understanding love is love, and that there's nothing wrong with being born different from someone else?

The better off we'll all be.

Love,

Dad

November 11

Hey Buddy...

I am in Colorado Springs, visiting one of my favorite comedy clubs, Loonee's. I don't often mention what club I am working when I tell you where I am, because in my mind I'm talking about work, and work won't interest you. But, if ever you wonder, ask. Ask and I will tell you the joys of Roger in Ann Arbor, Pete in Cuyahoga Falls, Mark in Rochester, and Erik here in Colorado. They are a rarity in my world: club owners that actually enjoy comedy.

(All too often, comedy club owners are interested in liquor sales first, getting stoned second, trying to bang their employees third, and original comedy somewhere down the line after that.)

Looking back over my notes, I realized that I told you about the trip Mommy and I took to not be on television, but I didn't share the story that captured the talk show's attention in the first place.

It all started with my friend Brad, who hit me up with the following: "Can I ask you a personal question? Feel free to say no."

I find such leads interesting, because nine-point-nine times out of ten, I have no problem giving the information being requested. Maybe my concept of "guarded information" differs from that of most people, or maybe it is others who worry too much about what's considered public or private information.

Regardless, as that precursor to the actual question was asked of me, I nodded amiably; I was indeed game for the coming inquisition. In other words: bring it.

"I take it your wife makes more than you do..." Brad began, and then trailed off.

Part of me wanted to correct him. Not on the assumption, that was dead on. Mommy is absolutely the bigger breadwinner in our family. What I wanted to correct was the format of his sentence, and say, "That's not really a question, it's more a cautious hanging statement, where you stop talking and wait for me to verify your belief, because you're too meek to actually ask what you want to know."

I understand polite, but I don't understand timidity. If you're going to ask something normally considered "rude," then ask it. Diluting offense doesn't actually work.

Now, all that said, in no way was I bothered by either the assumption or the question. Mommy has a master's degree from an accredited university. She has been working her way up the professional ladder since graduating with her bachelor's, and was even an adjunct professor. So of course she earns more than an unknown comedian. Anyone who would believe otherwise has not thought things through very well.

This income disparity doesn't offend or bother me; in fact, I've never understood the male preoccupation with being financially dominant in a relationship.

When it comes to the basic necessities, I pull my weight; our bills are split down the center 50/50. I leech in no way. But there are limited occasions where she absorbs the cost of an expense. We call those instances "her wants." There are home improvement ideas she has that do not interest me in the least, and her sister

254

set her on a path of little resistance regarding these situations. She told Mommy that sometimes it's just not worth it to argue over something.

For example, if Mommy believes that the yard needs more flowers, while I couldn't care less about flowers, it's easier for her to just buy everything using her own money. That way, when the monthly bills arrive I don't get irritated and bellow: "Why in God's Great Name — pause for genuflection, praise Him — did we spend $50 at Lowe's!?"

Not that this approach hasn't bitten her in the butt on occasion. For the longest time, she wanted to own a king-size mattress, a purchase I was firmly against.

Mommy likes to sprawl out at night. It is as if she cannot find peace unless situated diagonally across the bed, with one arm stretched out above her head, the other extended to the side, and both legs flailing haphazardly wherever they may fall. Add to this situation the fact that Kitty has to be touching me at all times while he sleeps, and you'd think that I was the one begging for extended space.

Nope.

When I sleep, I'm pretty much in corpse mode. I sleep on the very edge of my side of the bed, taking up exactly the width of my body in space, and no more. I wasn't sure how getting a larger mattress would change anything, but I was willing to listen to Mommy's reasoning.

She devised a plan: the purchase would come out of her bank account, and if I enjoyed the mattress, then I could pitch in and pay her back for my portion. She did some advance research, brought me to the store, and I reiterated my stance: "I'm against buying anything new." I then gave my opinion of each mattress,

255

choosing both the softest (and unfortunately most expensive) of the lot.

Mommy threw down her credit card; our bedroom was rearranged to create optimal living space and a sense of functional feng shui, and we settled in.

As expected, I was granted the edge of the bed, just as before. Mommy sprawled out in enjoyment; Kitty stretched himself out along the width of my body, leaving me nowhere to move. Basically, I went from lying on the edge of a small bed, to lying on the edge of a huge bed.

When the bill for the new mattress came due, I smiled and said, "This one's on you, sweetie."

She pouted, but paid it in full.

To be fair, now that you and Sister like to climb in with us, having a king-size mattress is a lifesaver. Sister likes to snuggle up against me, robbing Kitty of his perch, and you like to either touch Mommy or sleep sideways between us, kicking me with your feet and head-butting Mommy as we try to get comfortable.

For the record, things do fall in her favor. When I wanted a nice iPod docking station, I didn't ask her to chip in just because she might use it every so often. In that case, music was more important to me. We picked out a speaker together, and I threw down the cash alone.

So I'm fine with Mommy earning more than me.

I pay my half of all the important bills, and continue to save for the future on the side. I think she put it best herself, once, when she called me her "little school teacher."

"You may not be an investment banker, pulling in six figures a year," she explained, "but you make about as much as if I had married a small-town teacher. Plus, you make people laugh, and do what you love. That's worth a lot."

I don't know how I got so lucky as to find Mommy and have her fall in love with me, but when you enter into relationships, always remember what's important.

Yes, having enough money is important. But define "enough." Don't worry about always having what's new or "best." Keep your eye on being happy.

Most importantly, be in love.

Love,

Dad

November 19

Hey Buddy...

We are in Madison, Wisconsin, visiting Graw Janet and Bada Joe. You've been hanging out with your cousin Moose, and having a blast.

You'll probably know why you don't have a younger sibling by the time you read this, but if that's not the case, here's the story.

When it was time to start our family, Mommy and I made a discovery: we couldn't make babies the old fashioned way.

Mommy wasn't ovulating. Her eggs, though healthy, wouldn't pop out of the ovary and into the fallopian tube for fertilization. My sperm, for that matter, couldn't fertilize anything even if they found an egg. Sperm needs to be both plentiful, and a specific shape. Large numbers, because so many don't make the entire journey to the egg. Pointed heads, because they need to pierce that egg to create an embryo.

My swimmers have flat heads. They can bump up against an egg all they want, but in reality could never pierce one.

After rounds of medicated cycles, timed ovulation shots, and intrauterine inseminations — the turkey baster method — it was time for IVF: in vitro fertilization.

Our hospital was able to harvest twenty eggs, and fertilize eleven thanks to a process that used a needle to place my sperm directly into the egg for nestling. Mommy and I were exceedingly lucky in that three transfers became two babies: you and Sister. Our first transfer failed, but after that we were given Sister, and the very first attempt for our second child provided you.

During the process, we inserted one embryo at a time, because neither of us were interested in Octo-momming our way to a Brady Bunch from the starting gate. Since the math on IVF is never one-to-one—some embryos don't survive the thaw, others don't mature properly—we had three healthy embryos remaining. Three embryos, in deep freeze, waiting.

But waiting... for what?

For many reasons, Mommy and I knew we were stopping at two children. After having Sister, we knew that one more would be the magic number. Parenting is difficult enough when it's two parents, one kiddo. Evening things up—two parents, two kids—while an exponential increase on paper, is actually several times more difficult than double coverage. Having more children than parents? At that point, we'd be tearing our hair out.

Plus, you have to keep in mind my work schedule: I travel. A lot.

When you and Sister gang up on Mommy it's bad enough, she's already ready for a padded room by the end of a weekend. But adding another to the fray? One more would push Mommy over the edge.

Add in our respective ages and the financial responsibilities of more kids, and it made nothing but sense to stop at two.

That, however, left us with several embryos remaining. What were we going to do with those?

Our options were:

- Throw them away. Some people equate the disposal of embryos to abortion, but I cannot go down that path. Abortion is such a heated, personal topic that I don't want to broach it, but I do not see any parity between disposing of frozen cells and the termination of life. It's way too broad. Instead, I see waste. To destroy something that could be used for good is pathetic. Wasting them wasn't an option. But it's not murder.
- Continue to store them. Our family was complete; two kiddos was the plan, so storage seemed like an unnecessary financial burden.
- Donate them to stem cell research. This was a decision to be made carefully. On the one hand, donation to research could do a lot of good for humanity. On the other, it would anger knee-jerk, blinder-driven people who believe a clump of cells invisible to the naked eye is "life." So... win-win. Due to these two factors, this was almost the path we took.
- Donate them to a couple even more infertile than we were. Wait, we could donate embryos? Give someone else the opportunity to start a family of their own? Once we discovered this path, there was no looking back.

Though Mommy and I can't get naked and make babies, we still have the ability to create children with our genes. There are couples out there for whom biological babies isn't an option. With embryo donation, we could give our baby starter kits to a couple, allowing them to create the family they longed for. We would be granting hope to people bereft of it.

Mommy and I didn't donate to be generous, and we didn't do it for good karma. We did it because it was the right thing to do. We had the ability to help someone, so we did. End of story. Knowing how difficult our meager struggle was, we could only imagine how painful it would be for someone in a worse predicament.

If the decision to donate was step one, picking a home for our embryos was step two. That was a doozy.

We wanted to take part in "known adoption," and not just throw our embryos to the wind. Mommy didn't want to live with the questions: Did my embryos create life? Will I pass my biological child in the grocery store someday and not know it? Personally, I worried about you or Sister winning the Alabama Lottery. I didn't want either of you wandering into a bar in twenty-odd years, meeting someone you were instantly attracted to without knowing why, and… well, you get the drift. A one in a million possibility, but hey, I want to protect you as much as absolutely possible.

Mommy and I were put in touch with a small agency designed to match donors to recipients. A boutique agency, if you will, as opposed to "Donating Embryos Inc." I was surprised to discover that matching embryo donors and recipients can be quite the little niche business. There's profit aplenty to be had off desperate people, which I find repulsive. I understand a finder's fee; I'm not so keen on meeting sales goals. So we went small and personal over corporate.

Once signed up with the matchmaker, a new wrinkle appeared in the process. People are judgmental creatures; studies show we make snap decisions about others in the blink of an eye. We judge by appearance, speech patterns, hair color, eye color, skin color… anything and everything we can. I didn't realize how quickly (and possibly unfairly) Mommy and I dismissed possible recipients. To put it bluntly: I'd swear the first list of offerings we saw was straight from the "People of Walmart" website.

Am I horrible for saying that? Yes.

Am I going to hide it and pretend to be a better person than I am? No.

There's currently a dating app called Tinder; it's based on swiping left or right on a snap judgment. See someone you like? Swipe right. See someone you find unattractive? Swipe left. That's what looking at perspective recipients felt like: Tinder for Parenting. For every "maybe," there were a handful of immediate "NO" reactions. And the "maybe" was never strong, it was just "well, in comparison to..."

Some were easy. There were the couples who had children from respective former marriages, but wanted to have their own kids together. To us, someone trying for their first baby took precedent over someone that already had children to love. There were the couples, and again forgive the honesty, who were recently married and looking to start their families in their late 40s and early 50s. Was it ageist of us to pass them over? Yes. Did we do it anyway? Yes.

Mommy and I felt guilty; judging others is never a positive feeling. Going back to my "People of Walmart" analogy: when you look at that site, you have an innocent chuckle because someone is dressed inappropriately, or has crazy hair. But when you see someone on an "I need embryos to start my family" website, you know there is love, hope, and longing behind the inappropriate clothes, excessive weight, and crazy hair.

Fortunately, Mommy's therapist came to our rescue. She put into words what we could not: we wanted someone like us. Not too young—"I'm nineteen and want to start a family!"—and not too old.

("55 and infertile" may make for a great headline on "CougarsOnly.com," but not on a fertility website).

We wanted a couple that was both loving, and progressive. If your bio read: "We're a loving heterosexual couple, just like the Bible wants!" you could expect to be passed over.

(We were not offered any same-sex couples, but that could have been the direction we went had one arose.)

Eventually, we settled on a nice, middle-class Midwestern couple. The women-folk clicked immediately in areas only women click in, and the other husband and I clicked in our male disinterest in conversation and all things touchy-feely. They're such nice people, we even forgave them for being Vikings fans.

(It could be worse; they could like the Bears.)

This "connection of the couples" first took place in November 2014. It was followed by months of medical exams, psychological exams, lawyer-reviewed contracts, medical testing, and money-raising.

(While we were technically donating our embryos, there were still medical costs aplenty for them to overcome. Our recipients, sadly, did not have the same rock star insurance Mommy does. Fortunately, we chose them for their personalities, not their bank accounts.)

Now comes the part of our story, that gets a little bit sad... none of the embryos made it.

Over the course of a year all three survived their thaw and were transferred, but all three failed to take hold. So, while there was once a possibility you'd have a non-traditional sibling out there, it did not come to pass.

(The good news is that Mommy and the woman became good friends, and remain so to this day.)

Fortunately, you and Sister absolutely adore one another. Yes, I know, that will change as you grow. Hell, it will probably disappear by the time you become teenagers, but right now

Mommy and I enjoy watching you two play so much that it melts our hearts. You two interact so tenderly; you run around, read books together, do stunts together — the other day you two lined up all our dining room chairs, then balance-walked across them and leapt over the back of the couch. It wasn't the safest thing in the world, but you two were on a tear and I couldn't bring myself to interrupt it in the name of security.

I'm sure there will be points where you wish you had a younger brother or sister, but these are the cards you've been dealt.

Appreciate them.

Love,

Dad

November 26

Hey Buddy...

In addition to yapping jokes into a microphone on stage, I enjoy jotting my thoughts down pen-to-paper. I blog, have a weekly column on a website called The Good Men Project, and every so often drop something on a website called The Huffington Post. And, of course, I am compiling this series of scribblings to you.

I also submit my work anywhere and everywhere I think it might get published, because I'm forever trying to get my name out there in the hopes of gaining a little public recognition. Not for my ego, but so that I can put butts in seats at comedy clubs. I want people to say, "Hey, I know that guy. I like his writing. I should go see him perform."

(Because the more I'm known, the more I can work, and the more I work the better I can provide for you and Sister.)

To that end, I've been submitting to a noted publication called The Atlantic. It's a 160-year-old magazine that is highly regarded by fans of quality writing. If I were to get an article in there, it would be quite a feather in my cap, so to speak.

The other day, an associate from The Atlantic sent me the nicest rejection letter I have ever had the pleasure of reading. Here are a couple of sentences:

Nathan,

I'm Nick, one of the younglings at The Atlantic who has the role of managing the general submissions@ inbox. It's a flood, and we accept very, very little from it (most of our commissioned and freelance pieces come through editors or submissions inboxes specific to the sections).

I mention this because in several dozen thousand submissions I've gone through, I really like yours and they stick out.

That last sentence really jumped out at me.

I'll admit, I read it a half dozen times, because it's a damn fine ego boost. "In several dozen thousand submissions I've gone through, I really like yours and they stick out."

He went on to explain that I was being rejected because while my writing is compelling, the content isn't exactly a fit for The Atlantic.

It makes me wonder: what defines success? I don't know, actually. This isn't something I'm going to answer for you; I'm writing to try and figure it out myself.

According to this insider, I'm a better writer than "dozens of thousands." How insane is that? It's a big compliment, which is positive. But, the letter was also a rejection, which is negative. The editor also gave me his personal email address and asked me to submit directly to him in the future.

That's more than 99% of submitters get.

Overall, I'm not sure what to make of it. On the one hand, compliments feed the ego. On the other, food feeds the body, and compliments don't buy food.

There's a saying: money isn't everything.

I've heard it a million times, and a few weeks ago I was listening to a podcast where an empire-building entrepreneur was doling out sage advice on being successful.

"Money isn't everything," he started. "Be happy. Find your happiness. Inner peace is what's important. I didn't realize that when I was younger."

Suddenly, I was angry.

Maybe mansions, cars, or a successful career didn't make him happy, but extreme wealth sure as hell made his life easier. As he hit middle age and looked back, he realized he sacrificed personal happiness while chasing dreams. Now that he's caught them, he's saying marriage and kids fulfill him. The problem is, of course he can meditate, exercise, eat organic food, and do yoga all day.

He's. Rich.

I wonder if he'd be as happy if he had a wife and kids he couldn't provide for, because he didn't have millions of dollars in the bank. Money can't buy happiness, but money takes away worry.

Worry, for the record, is a complete pain in the ass. Yes, it's possible for someone living paycheck to paycheck to be happy, but happy isn't a decision. You can make a conscious effort to think a certain way, or to focus on the good in life and not the negative, but "happy" doesn't just happen because you want it to. If you're worrying where your next meal is coming from, or if you'll make rent next month, it's slightly difficult to decide to "just be happy."

My life is an odd three-way split.

Personally, I'm happy. I love you, Sister, and Mommy like nobody's business. Everyone is healthy, and I couldn't ask for more. Professionally, I'm fractured. When I'm on stage, I'm ecstatic. Nothing beats my job. But when I'm sending out my CV in search of the next gig or contacting a club I've already worked and done really well and getting radio silence in response, it's horrible.

They say, "Do what you love and you'll never work a day in your life," but that's a lie. I love what I do, but it is work. And hard work kinda sucks, even if the rewards make it worth it. Maybe better advice would be that life is about balance. Do what you do, and put your heart and soul into it, but remember your blessings. Sure, my work is difficult, but my family makes the effort worth it.

Which brings me back to the compliment-slash-rejection. If anything, it's fuel to keep moving forward. Because that's what I have to do: move forward, head down, into the wind. For you, Sister, and my sanity. Always with crossed fingers and heavy effort.

Hopefully there is a payday out there at the end of all this.

Love,

Dad

November 28

Hey Buddy…

Today was an interesting mix of good and awful.

Several weeks ago, one of the most prominent booking agents in the comedy world referred me to a management company in Los Angeles. He said I could use his name to get my foot in the door.

Mommy and I wrote up what we thought was a solid introduction letter. Not an email, an actual letter. Old-school style.

We put it in a box with a little, "Hey, we researched you, so here's a little swag from your alma mater," and sent it off First Class mail. Two days later, post office tracking showed our package had been delivered. We waited. And waited. And waited. Over two weeks passed. The manager ignored our introduction; he didn't respond with either interest or thanks.

So, I reached out via email and offered a kind, "Hi, I'm following up on a package I sent your way…"

I got a one-sentence response. He half-asked for some video, but seemed more annoyed than curious.

I sent him a link to a video of mine; his reply was a basic admittance he didn't understand how links worked. Instead of clicking on it and watching my video, he said he couldn't figure it out.

I walked him through everything—"Move cursor over link; click. Watch video."—and heard nothing for over a week.

He finally emailed me back today while you and Sister were napping.

It was an indifferent rejection. The way his note read was almost as if he either didn't watch my set, or watched it while doing something else and barely paid attention. He never mentioned the introductory letter, my recommendations, or my jokes.

In short, he asked what my "hook" was.

Having original material and a unique voice wasn't enough for him; in this business, you need a "hook." Do you have a catchphrase, a repeated refrain you sprinkle throughout your set? Even if your comedy is uninspired and lacks originality, if you say something after each joke that people can latch onto, they will remember that signature slogan and launch you to the top of the stratosphere. Or maybe you're socially unique—a left-handed orphan raised by wolves, or someone born with six fingers on each hand. Those are selling points; something that can be sold on paper without examining actual skills.

He was looking for something to pitch. What was my angle? Because in the world of stand-up comedy, being funny isn't an angle anymore.

I think the most angering aspect is how poorly written the rejection was. The manager confused "your" and "you're," and "there" and "their." When I forwarded the email to Mommy, she was so confused by his inarticulate response she responded, "I don't get it... what is he saying?" The word salad the manager barfed up was so poorly written, Mommy couldn't make sense of it. I had to tell her he was passing on me.

This might leave you wondering, "Do you really want someone like that representing you?"

The answer is yes. And no. I mean... right now I have no one in my corner. And as it stands, people like him are the gatekeepers to power. They guard the passageways to those who can put you on television and get you booked in great clubs.

The people in power don't want to be inundated by the unwashed masses, meaning people like me. They use people like the manager I contacted as buffers. You generally need to use a manager or an agent to hook up with someone who can put you in front of a camera.

(Trust me, I've reached out to those in power many times. Silence is the response I got.)

Anyway, the entire incident left me frustrated, angry, and admittedly a little depressed. No one likes rejection, and even more so when it's done with a lack of respect.

After the rejection, I looked up the manager's client list, and that made everything worse. I realized I had worked with someone on his roster a couple years ago; they were my opening act and struggled all weekend. Each of their shows was mediocre, with the audience not laughing because the material wasn't interesting.

When I got on stage, however, I got big laughter and applause. When his client was on stage I would wonder, "Is this a dead audience?" only to discover, "Nope. They were just waiting for someone funny."

I have to admit that it swelled my ego every show; I thought I was hot shit.

If there's one thing I've been able to take pride in regarding my career, it's the compliments I've received from people who work at the comedy clubs where I perform. When a manager, bartender, or doorperson tells me, "I see a lot of comedians, and dude, you're good," it means something. When I get told, "You're different from everything I see," I am humbled.

My favorite compliment came from a doorman in Cleveland. After my show, he said, "I've been here a year and can guess the punchlines of most of the comedians that come through. You? Not so much. You surprise me. I like that."

I write all that because...

...well, in all honesty, I'm trying to feel good about myself. Thinking of the manager's rejection, the way he did it without taking even the most cursory examination of me or my comedy...

I need to latch on to the accolades I've received.

A year after feeling like hot shit for being "better" than the manager's comedian, that comedian was on TV; the manager got his client on one of the top late-night talk shows.

Suddenly, the fact I had bested them in a small club didn't mean much. My ego had run amok that weekend, but the other comedian trounced me in the greatest of ways and was on to bigger and better things. Today, that comic is getting prime slots across the country. Meanwhile, I'm fighting with 100 other comedians for a gig at a Moose Lodge in Nowhere, Iowa.

Anyway, after reading the rejection email, I just sat, staring at my computer screen.

Rejection hurts. Comedy is about putting your thoughts, your ideas out there. Having those thoughts, those feelings ignored or dismissed hurts.

When given criticism, you must digest what has been said; you always have room for improvement. But sometimes the judgment passed on you is an expression of that person's limitations, not an assessment of your abilities.

So, that was the awful part of the day.

About fifteen minutes after I received the email, you woke up.

I've mentioned this before, but you don't wake up easily. You generally wander out of your bedroom rubbing your eyes. Your hair sticks out at all angles. You shuffle as you walk. You're generally looking for love, and for the most part you want Mommy, but every so often I'll do.

Today you came out holding your water bottle as if it was a security blanket. Your eyes were squinting. You saw me and shuffled over; I was lying on the couch, staring at the ceiling and stewing.

You crawled up onto me, laid your head down on my chest, and snuggled in deep. And for a moment, everything went away. For a moment, everything was OK.

You weren't trying to make me feel better; you were just trying to take in the world around you. "I was asleep… Daddy is here… I'm not ready to play yet… I just want to lie down for a few more minutes… on Daddy."

You weren't trying to make me feel better, but you did. You snuggling up to me took all the anger away, at least for a while. A smoker doesn't quit cigarettes because they put one patch on their arm, but it lessens the craving. That's what you were to me in that moment: a patch. You helped me refocus on what's important. You. Sister. Mommy. Kitty. Our family.

(Maybe Simon.)

Today was one step forward, two steps back. Or maybe it's all even. I don't know.

I didn't have a manager before; I don't have a manager now. Maybe the hope it was all about to get easier, or better, is what made today feel so defeating.

I tell you this, though: through everything, all the ups and downs of my career, Mommy has been there.

There is an old saying: Behind every good man is a great woman.

I think that's nonsense.

Mommy has never been behind me. She has been by my side: my partner, my equal, my better. She has been out in front of me, cajoling me forward, encouraging me during times like this when I've just been kicked in the teeth or made to feel like what I do doesn't matter.

"I believe in you."

That's what Mommy tells me.

"I believe in you."

Those four words are sometimes the most important things I hear.

276

When it comes time for you to marry, marry well. Learn what you can from my mistakes, but absolutely learn from the one thing I did right: find someone who supports you and who you can support in return. Never date or marry out of desperation or the idea, "Well, this is good enough."

Find your partner, your equal, your better. Find that person, that anchor, and tether yourself to them. Love them with all your heart. Make sure that you have a sanctuary to return to, a place you can exist where everything is OK personally, even when things are askew professionally.

Yes, being rejected felt like a kick in the gut. It always does. But you, Sister, and Mommy carry me through the tough times.

I used to want success because I wanted recognition for my thoughts and ideas. Now? Now I just want to provide for you and Sister. I don't want either of you to want for anything.

There is an old saying about no door being closed without a window of opportunity being opened in response.

The manager closed that door and locked it. I'm just waiting for my window.

Love,

Dad

July 5

Hey Buddy…

As I write this post script, several months after my final letter, you are about to turn three.

I'm glad I wrote the notes to you and Sister when I did. I tended to capture ages where you are tiny and adorable. If I wrote during later years, say ages three to four, it would involve numerous instances of "Today you threw a fit because…" followed by a ton of responses, including (but not limited to):

- I turned off the TV.
- You had to go to bed.
- Mommy didn't take off her coat quickly enough.
- Mommy didn't put on her coat quickly enough.
- You couldn't have cereal for lunch.
- You couldn't have cereal for snack.
- You couldn't have cereal for dinner.
- Seriously, what is it with you and cereal?

As you approach the existence of a threenager, it's frustratingly hilarious. You've become the most bossy little biddy on the planet, so much so that Mommy has taken to calling you Kim Jung Truman, because by all measures you are a tiny dictator.

Everything in your life has to be done "just so." On your bed are two blankets; one blue, the other brown. When you are put to bed at night, the blue one has to be laid over your body, feet to neck. Then the brown one has to be folded in half and put over your feet. If this doesn't happen, you aren't going to bed. You sit up, and start admonishing us, saying, "No, no, no, no… brown blanket, feet," and giving a series of other orders to follow.

You will also only eat cereal out of the yellow bowl, and only do so while using the blue spoon. Any other bowl or spoon elicits frustration that soon turns to anger if we do not acquiesce to your demands quickly enough.

You've also begun the curious habit of toy hoarding. It's delightfully entertaining.

There are three points in the day when you simply must have your little hands stuffed with just about every toy you can carry: bedtime, waking/breakfast, and going to daycare.

At those moments in time, you'll carry a multitude of cars, plastic hammers, or stuffed animals. When you wake in the morning, you remember exactly what you went to sleep with, and you won't leave your bed until you have them all with you. If one has slipped down the side of the bed or remains under a blanket, you'll look for it.

"Where blue car?" you'll ask repeatedly, your fists already full of plenty of other cars.

Only after the final car has been located will you allow yourself to be carried out.

The other day, I got this text from Mommy: "When we got to daycare, he wanted to bring in his backhoe and the Dinoco race car. I talked him out of bringing in his shark water bottle, but once we got inside the building he changed his mind about the water bottle and started flailing on the floor, kicking the door. I carried him outside to get the water bottle and discovered another race car, the blue one, which had apparently been under his butt the whole ride, and now we had to bring that one, too.

He's getting really good at carrying a ton of shit at once. Last night he took two cars and THAT HUGE DUMP TRUCK into bed with him. He slept with it all in there, too. This morning he immediately started rummaging through the blankets to find the taxi, because it had fallen down the side of the bed. Thankfully, we found it quickly."

Bedtime is one hell of a routine with you, for the record.

Your favorite song is "The One Moment," by OK Go. I have to sing it to you every night, like a lullaby. If it comes on when we're in the car, you shout "Color Band!" — your name for them — and begin shouting out all the colors as they appear in the video.

Then we sing "Roxanne," "Every Little Thing She Does is Magic," and "Can't Stand Losing You," by The Police.

(I'm not much for lullabies. Not because I don't like them, I just don't know the words to any. I'm probably repeating myself here, but oh well.)

We've been doing this for months, and lately you've been singing along with me. You know most of the words to every song, and I have to admit it is Goddamned amusing to hear you intone, "I guess you'd call it suicide, but I'm too full, to swallow my pride..."

You're at a particularly loving stage in life, and your current modus operandi to avoid bedtime is to become particularly snuggly, demanding hugs and kisses. And not just any hugs and kisses, you have specific ways of giving and receiving affection.

"Want chair hug," you'll whimper.

There's a child's poofy chair next to your toddler bed; it's the perfect height to sit in and hold your hand at bedtime.

281

So I'll sit in the chair, and you'll crawl from your bed into my arms, lay your little head down on my shoulder, and receive a "chair hug." Then there are floor hugs ("Lay down, Daddy."), pick me up hugs, bed hugs...

The list is seemingly endless.

And don't get me started on the kisses. First we'll exchange a regular kiss goodnight, then you start in with "Kiss forehead. Kiss ear. Kiss other ear. Kiss eye. Kiss other eye. Kiss cheek..." You get the picture. Oh, and after all that is finished? "Hold hand one minute. One minute hold hand..."

Yes, after all the hugging and kissing and singing, we have to sit and hold hands in silence. Which, I have to admit, is awesome.

And it's impossible to deny. I can't be a hard ass and say, "Bed!" in a firm voice when snuggle-bug little you is avoiding slumber because of affection. It's not like you're asking for time with the iPad or to watch PBS Kids or something non-conducive to sleep.

Every night as we move through the routine, the thought crosses my mind, "I wish I could freeze you at this age, right here, right now."

I want to capture everything there is about you at age two and a half. The cute way you wobble when you walk, the way you shake your whole body when you get excited about something... everything.

And it's not just you; Sister is four and a half, and I have the same "Freeze! Right now, just stop growing!" thoughts about her. Every time she does something age appropriate, like the way she says. "I missed you." She makes it into a two-syllable word, miss-ed. It sounds like "misted." Whenever I pick her up from daycare or when I return home from a business trip, it's "Daddy! I miss-ted you!"

Every time she says it my heart melts; it's so adorably wrong.

I was wondering if this attitude was healthy, when I had the opportunity to spend some time with an old acquaintance of mine, Jimmy. Like me, Jimmy is a stand-up comedian; he's the warm-up act for the Conan O'Brien Show.

Because of our careers, I hadn't seen him in nine years. That's when I left Los Angeles to be with Mommy. Whenever Jimmy would tour to the comedy club near me, I'd be off touring myself, and our paths wouldn't cross.

Until recently.

He was in town, I was in town, so I dropped by the club and made my way into the green room to catch up. The topic of discussion quickly became fatherhood and parenting, as it does when you have two parents in a room. While we waxed philosophic about our daddy duties, words exited Jimmy's mouth that made me smile.

"My son is nine," Jimmy started, and then he paused. He got a somewhat faraway look in his eyes, as if reflecting, before continuing. "My son is nine... and I wish, I wish I could just freeze him, right now, as he is."

Jimmy explained that his son was at a point in life where everything was just perfect. He was so wonderful, Jimmy enjoyed every moment with him, and he wanted it to go on like that forever.

As he spoke, I realized that since Sister's birth, I had been on a non-stop "hit the pause button!" train of thought. It wasn't that I wanted her to remain at the beautiful age of four and a half, where she said "miss-ted" instead of "missed," I also wanted her to remain a newborn at birth.

When she was just a month or two old, Sister was gassy and had problems sleeping. I'd gather her from her crib and lie on the couch all night, letting her sleep on my chest as she farted away her bubbly tummy. I'd be completely sleep deprived, yet giggling and laughing, "I wish I could just freeze you right now, and live like this forever."

Then she started toddling around the house, and I'd have the same thought: "Look at you, learning to walk... I wish I could freeze you right now..."

And so on.

It's the same with you. You have your own, unique-to-you milestones in life — "chair hug," "kiss nose" — and at each one my mind screams, "Just stop growing! Right now!"

Hearing Jimmy still having thoughts with his nine-year-old made me happy. Yes, these moments all disappear. They fade with time, never to be recaptured. But they're replaced by new moments, new developments, new stages in life. And you want to grab each one and never let it go.

Fortunately, Mommy is a wonderful scrapbooker.

On every birthday, she creates a year-in-review look back at you and Sister. Combined with these yearbooks, we have digital photos, videos, and every possible documentation needed to hold on to memories, even if the child standing before us is no longer two, twelve, or twenty.

Truth is, you will forever grow, and as parents we will forever wish, "If only we could freeze them, right now..."

And this will be, the one moment that matters at all.

Love,

Dad

"I'm a potty!"

Special Thanks

To my Mrs., one Lydia Fine.

She not only gave this book the first eyeballing as far as editing goes, she also designed both the front and back covers.

(She's good like that.)

Also thanks to Kristine Bjork, who now goes by the God-awful moniker "Roggentein," a name I refuse to acknowledge.

(Apologies to her husband, Reece.)

(Also: I've been informed the name is "Roggentien," not "Roggentein." This is just more proof "Bjork" is a better name, if you ask me.)

Kristine did the mop up on all this nonsense, and I tell you this: if this book contains an error, it's my fault, not hers. Because I am a stubborn mule, sometimes I just like the way something looks, or "sounds" in my head. Kristine probably saw and corrected a technical grammatical error, and then I went ahead and kept it the way I liked it. Because I'm dumb.

About the Author

Nathan Timmel has been writing since he could scribble using crayons. As a comedian, he has released five CDs — several of which are in rotation on Sirius/XM radio (as well as available for purchase on both iTunes and Amazon) — and toured both Iraq and Afghanistan for American troops stationed far from home.

Nathan currently lives in Iowa City with his wife, daughter, son, gender-confused kitty Simon, and doggy named "Kitty." He is an avid fan of Billy and the Boingers, and enjoys a fine pair of pants.

Nathan has written more nonsense than you can shake a stick at:

- I Was a White Knight... Once
- Touched by Anything but an Angel
- The Four Legged Perspective: One Dog's Take on Burp Rags and Baby Sisters
- An Inattention to Detail: A Comedian Lobs Jokes in Iraq.
- The Accidental Substitute: How a Stand Up Comedian Became a Part Time Teacher
- Same Same, Why Gay Doesn't Matter
- Go Home Happy: The Serious Side of Stand-Up Comedy
- Are You There, Xenu? It's Me, Nathan.
- It's OK to Talk to Animals (and Other Letters from Dad)

- The Bearded Midget (and other Asian adventures)

Please visit *nathantimmel.com* for anything and everything Nathan related, including his free, weekly podcast, but not his naked pictures. Those are available for only $19.95 a month on his alternate website, www.engorged...

You know what? Never mind.

Thanks for reading. Go see Nathan perform. You'll giggle and have a good time.

Promise.

Made in the USA
Lexington, KY
29 December 2018